Swing Tr

Making Sense Of Patterns And Capitalizing On Price Trends Using Actionable Technical Analysis, Chart Reading Tools, And Technical Indicators

Andrei D. Carlson

Table of Contents

Introduction

While many people invest for the long term, most are passive about it and let someone else handle their finances. Do you want someone else directing your wealth-building and financial growth, or would you rather take control yourself and grow wealth the way you want to do it? Are you looking for financial freedom, here and now, rather than waiting for 20 years or 30 years to see results?

If you want to be in control and achieve financial freedom, swing trading might be the kind of wealth-building you are looking for. Swing trading is very different from traditional investing. With swing trading, you are really creating a business to earn profits from the stock market in the present time. By earning profits now, you can achieve financial independence quickly, and once you do, it's possible to grow and expand your trading so that you can build wealth and not just earn an income. The potential profits with swing trading are, in principle, limitless. You can make any amount with a minimal amount of time and effort if you have the right tools, strategies and guiding principles at hand.

Of course, not everyone is suitable for swing trading, which is one of the reasons why I wrote this book. After learning what swing trading is in this book and how it works, as well as the techniques that are used by swing traders to earn profits, you can determine whether or not you want to try it. Many of you will move forward and succeed, and some will fail. Don't worry about which side of the ledger you sit on. It is better to try and fail than to not try at all. And if this is not something that ends up fitting your style and abilities, there are many other ways to make money on the financial markets that you can investigate, such as options trading, day trading, or even Forex. However, at least give it a reasonable shot before deciding what works for you. I hope this book will help you start your journey of financial success.

In this book you will learn what swing trading is, as well as how it differs from other methods of investing and trading. We'll see some real examples and learn what kinds of profits can be made on a trade, as well as how much money you need to start investing.

Then, we'll dive into the technical details of swing trading. It's important to understand that swing trading requires a bit of mathematical and financial analysis in order to estimate price movements on the markets accurately. This doesn't mean that you have to be some kind of math whiz, but you should be comfortable using graphs, charts, and mathematically based tools that help you estimate pricing shifts.

For those who find they are inclined to this type of work, we will give you a solid foundation that you can use to build on and start trading. Remember that one of the most important aspects of swing trading is that successful swing traders are always willing and ready to keep learning. So let's get started!

Chapter 1: Welcome To The World Of Swing Trading

The concept of swing trading is quite simple. Anyone who has paid attention to the stock markets at all realizes the fact that price movements on the markets are happening all the time. Sometimes, they seem random, with chaotic fluctuations that simply happen as people are trading. Sometimes, there are huge pricing shifts and adjustments in reaction to the big news about a given company or the stock market at large. Then, there are steady trends, which can be up or down and can last anywhere from a few days to weeks or even a year.

Swing Trading — Take Advantage Of The Swings

No matter what, there are always price swings on the stock market. The idea behind swing trading is extremely simple—you just trade on these swings. When the price is at a relatively low point, you buy the stock. Then, when the price swing happens and the price rises, you sell the stock and make a profit. That's it!

Of course, it's a lot more complicated than that. Otherwise, everyone would swing trade their way to millions of dollars. The key to swing trading is being able to recognize correctly when a price swing is getting started, and then you need to know the best moment to get in on a trade and when to exit a trade before the price peaks out and starts falling again.

Knowing these things is not magic—it's done using time-tested tools that stock traders have been relying on for nearly 100 years. With the advent of personal computing power, the tools have gotten more sophisticated, but the basic principles are the same. Learning how to use these tools and make profits is a mixture of study, research, and a bit of luck. It's as much art as it is science, and it does require that you develop a good sense of judgment, something that is basically going to come from getting a good education on the topic and from experience.

Swing trading can work the other way, too. That is, you don't have to rely on making profits from price increases in stocks, although that is probably the way that most traders will play the markets since we normally think in terms of profits from increasing prices. You can also "short" a stock and earn profits when a stock goes into a decline in pricing.

What Swing Traders Look For

The main thing that swing traders look for is getting in on a trend. A trend is a unidirectional pricing movement that can be either up or down, lasting for an extended period of time. Hence, it's a swing from a low price to a high price, or it's a swing from a high price to a low price. Trends can last for different lengths of time, but what a swing trader is looking for are trends that last days to weeks—or possibly months. The key to this strategy is knowing when to get in on the trend, as well as when to get out before it reverses (and stock prices always do). Of course, these trends are not uniform—the stock market is chaotic, and you are going to see many apparent trend reversals in stock market data. When you are looking back, it is easy to see that the long-term trend was moving in one direction strongly, but in the heat of the moment, it can be difficult to determine if a trend reversal is real, or if the main trend will resume. Part of learning how to be a good swing trader is learning the difference.

Swing traders also look for stocks that are ranging. For several extended time periods, stocks will be languishing, bouncing around between relative highs or lows, but never going below a certain point or breaking out to a higher price. Many stocks will do this for extended periods of time until some sort of news about the company, economic or political news, forces the price to break out. While the potential profits in the case of ranging stocks are not as good, you can still make solid profits. This provides a way to earn money at all times, not just when stocks are crashing or breaking out.

As a swing trader, you'll want to keep an eye on earnings calls. In many cases, earnings calls can cause a stock to either break out to a new higher level of pricing or crash to a new lower level. The price movements after earnings calls can be quite dramatic, and they can happen in both directions. In fact, in recent months, we've seen single day movements of $40 to $60 per share for some stocks. Taking advantage of earnings calls can be quite lucrative, but at the same time, they are going to require a lot of research and preparation beforehand. To earn profits from earnings calls, you're going to be studying the company in detail. You will also have to pay attention to economic and political news, and you'll need to keep an eye on the company's competitors. What they are going to can impact the fortunes of the company as much as the company's own financial health, by taking away or yielding market share.

Trading Vs. Investing

Before we continue, it's important for new swing traders to have a clear understanding of the differences between trading and investing. First, let's look at what investing really means. Instead of thinking of the stock market, think about your brother or aunt starting a business. They are looking for people to invest, and you are really excited about the business and believe it will be profitable, and so you kick in $10,000 for an ownership stake.

You are a part of the company – even if you are not directly involved in the day to day operations. If the company succeeds, you will gain financially, and if it fails, you might lose your $10,000 investment. In either case, you are probably going to be in the company for the long haul.

Investing in a publicly traded company is no different, even though it seems abstract and far removed. You invest in a company because you believe in that company and its long-term prospects. So people invest in companies on the stock market because they believe in the company and its future, and they are willing to tie themselves to the company. Think of the examples around us in the present market like Apple, Amazon, and Netflix. All companies that have solid long-term prospects and offer products and services that people can believe in. And they often get very passionate about it. Tesla is one such company, even though it makes no or weak profits, people who believe that electric cars are the future are betting on Tesla. Its high stock price demonstrates the passion of investors.

Of course, you can invest in mutual or index funds instead, so you can invest for the long-term without betting on a specific company. In that case, you are betting on a sector or the long-term behavior of the economy and stock market. So people can invest in the S & P 500.

In either case, the time horizon used by investors is long-term. At a minimum, they are looking to be in an investment for five years, and most are in for 10, 20, and even 30 years. The goal of the investment is to "buy and hold" investments you really believe in, whether it's a specific company or a stock market index. Ultimately, the goal is to grow wealth over time so that by retirement, you have enough funds that you can pull out to support a nice lifestyle without having to worry about money. When it comes to financial independence, for long-term investors, that is a goal—but it's a goal that is put off to the distant future. Long-term investors are looking to build up to it slowly but surely over time.

A trader takes a different approach. The trader does not really care about the long-term prospects of a company, or even the financial health of the company, although that may factor into some trading decisions. The main goal of a trader is to make cash profits now. So a trader is looking to profit on price movements of stocks. Even bad stocks have a lot of price movement. So trading in blue-chip companies is not necessarily something a trader looks for. Although if there are signs that the stock of a blue-chip company is going to move, a trader will certainly take advantage of it.

Trading is not investing, it's a for-profit business, with the goal of making profits in the here and now.

Speculation

For some, the term "speculation" has negative connotations. Speculation means you are trading stocks based on the belief that the price of the stock is going to move in one way or another. Of course, speculation is something that can be applied to any asset, so think of gold when you think of speculation. Speculation means that you're going to buy gold based on the belief (or hope) that the price of gold is going to rise.

Long-term investors and financial advisors often look down on speculation, thinking of it in terms of gambling. However, they don't really understand how swing traders speculate. First of all, swing traders are not "guessing" or hoping that the price of a stock is going to move in one direction or another. Rather, swing traders use time-tested techniques of analysis to study the behavior of stock prices. These methods help traders make estimates of price movements that are based on probability. When something is based on probability, obviously, it's not going to be right all the time. The goal of being a good trader is to have more wins than losses, and that is not something you are going to be able to achieve by guessing or playing around. You're not going to be entering into random trades as a swing trader, hoping that stock prices are going to be rising, you are going to study stocks and market movements carefully, and use the appropriate tools to determine the best time to get into a trade. This is an educated move based on study and analysis, not the kind of guessing game that long-term investors and some financial advisors imagine trading to be. Keep in mind that many people who talk down about trading have their own self-interests at heart. They are hoping to earn commissions and fees from people that use them for advice in their own investment plans.

Swing Trading Vs. Day Trading

We have generally defined what swing trading is, but day trading seeks to profit from price movements in the stock market as well. In fact, day traders are looking for the same trends or price swings, and they will use the same tools of analysis. Understanding the difference between day trading and swing trading will bring one of the most important aspects of swing trading to your attention.

Day traders are making trades that they enter into and exit on the same trading day. A day trader never holds their position overnight. In fact, the kinds of stocks that day traders typically trade, or the kinds of trades they enter into could wipe out their accounts if they held them overnight. This can happen due to after-hours trading or from the fast price movements that happen at the market open each morning. A day trader may enter into several trades in a day, looking to get in and out of the trades over the course of a few hours. Day traders can trade any kind of stock, but they usually trade stocks that are very volatile.

Volatility is a measurement of how often stock prices change and how large the price swings are. The more volatile a stock, the more likely a day trader can profit from it, since a volatile stock might move a lot during a single trading day, offering many opportunities for profits.

Any stock can be volatile, and some very popular stocks from big companies have a lot of volatility, but many of the stocks with the most volatility are pretty undesirable. Penny stocks are often very volatile, and trading penny stocks might be something that a day trader is interested in doing, looking for quick profits over a few hours.

Swing traders hold their positions overnight. So at the very least, swing traders will be looking for a pricing trend that lasts a day or two. In many cases, swing traders will hold their positions for days, a week, several weeks, or even a few months. Think of swing trading as the lazy man's method of day trading. Since swing trading has no specific time frame, other than making trades that are at least held overnight and probably less than six months in length, it's actually a fairly relaxed and flexible trading style. You can trade as often as you like, and you can hold positions until you feel comfortable getting out of them. There are no hard and fast rules.

Day trading is a pressure cooker lifestyle. That's why when you think about "day trading," the image of someone sitting at a bank of four or five computer screens all buzzing with charts or spreadsheets of numbers is what comes to mind. A day trader must devote full-time attention to their craft when the markets open, and this is also going to require a lot of study either the night before or early in the morning before markets open so that the day trader knows what trades to make.

In contrast, a swing trader can trade full-time if they want to, but it's not a requirement. Since you hold your positions overnight, you can only work on your trades at night or for a couple of hours during the day. Many swing traders hold full-time jobs and swing trade on the side. But you can devote more time to it if you want to and you can grow your business as large as you want as well. Swing trading also gives you more flexibility as to the types of stocks that you are likely to trade. So swing traders are often trading blue-chip stocks, provided that they are either entering a trend of some kind or ranging as we described earlier. The truth is virtually every stock is going to be doing this over some time frame, so you can study stocks and find the time frames that work best for you and buy and sell them when it makes sense.

Day trading is high pressure, and it's also high-risk. As a result, day trading is something that is highly regulated by the U.S. Securities and Exchange Commission (SEC). In order to day trade, you're required to have a margin account, and it needs a net asset value of $25,000 (so you need to deposit $25,000 cash, and then have a combination of cash and stocks worth that amount). The SEC has also defined what they call a "pattern day trader." Anyone can make the occasional day trade, and as a swing trader there, might be times here and there when making a day trade makes sense. But if you make four-day trades in any five-day period (a day being markets open, or business days), then you are labeled a pattern day trader. Your broker will enforce the rules and might require you to deposit enough funds in your account to meet the requirements. Day traders are at risk of a margin call, which means they might have losses that are greater than the value of their account. When there is a margin call, you have to deposit cash to cover your losses. So if you are not ready for all this, avoid making day trades.

Swing trading is lightly regulated, and in fact, it's not really regulated any more than any other type of stock trading. You are just considered a regular stock trader when you are doing swing trading. There are no minimum deposit requirements, and you can have a margin account or not have a margin account. All of that is up to you. Swing trading is risky, like any type of investing is risky. There is always a risk of loss of capital when you invest. But swing trading is far less risky than day trading.

Swing Trading Styles

Swing traders can vary in style, or they can have a mixture of styles. Some swing traders are trading slowly, looking for long term trends they can profit on, and these might last over the course of several months. Others might be short-term traders, specializing in trades that only last a day or two. Within each of these possibilities, people might approach things generally, looking to profit from any price swings, while others will specialize in ranging stocks or only look for longer-term trends. Styles can also vary by the types of stocks traded. You can trade blue-chip stocks, penny stocks (although that is less likely for a swing trader), specialize in a certain sector like tech or finance, or you might be willing to trade any stock. Your style might vary with time. Swing trading is entirely flexible, and you can basically do what you want.

Tools Used By Swing Traders

There are many tools used by swing traders, and we are going to be discussing them throughout the book. Here we will simply introduce them so that you have an idea of what they are. The first tool used is the stock chart. You can view stock charts like line charts, bar charts, or using a specialized tool called a candlestick chart. Most swing traders (and day traders) use candlestick charts so that they can get a handle on pricing information since this is what candlestick charts provide. Don't worry if you haven't heard about candlestick charts before—we will be talking about this in detail in a future chapter.

Second, there are many analysis tools used by swing traders. The purpose of these tools is to estimate when a stock is going to undergo a shift in the current trend. So, for example, you are seeing a stock declining in price, but then there are signals in the data that prices are going to start increasing because there are signs people are starting to buy into the stock again.

Candlestick charts are one indicator used for this purpose, but people also look toward certain chart patterns that have been identified by experts to signal coming price trend shifts. These are old rules of thumb, many of which were developed in the 1930s.

Most traders use more sophisticated, mathematically based tools to help remove guessing from the equation. These include moving averages and indicators that will help you determine if stocks are overbought or oversold. Don't worry if you don't understand this right now—we are going to be gradually introducing all of this throughout the book.

Types Of Stock Market Charts

As a swing trader, you are going to be pretty focused on what type of charts you are using for analysis of your trades. There are going to be times when one type is more useful than another. The most basic type of chart is the one that most people are familiar with, a simple line chart. Here is an example:

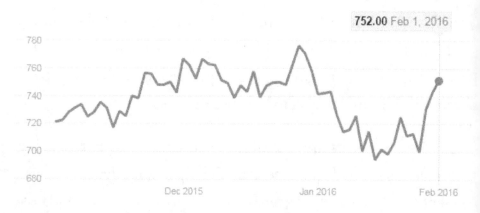

So it's a basic graph that shows the price of a stock over time. While people in the industry get obsessed with things like candlesticks, a line chart has its uses. I recommend using line charts when you are trying to look for price reversal signals like double tops and head and shoulders (we will be discussing these later). They come out clearly in line charts, but of course, you are free to stick to one time of chart for your purposes.

The second major type of chart is called a bar chart. This is a primitive form of a candlestick chart. Bar charts divide up a trading session into blocks of time and give you information about whether or not the price rose or fell during the trading session, and what the high and low prices were.

A bar chart is going to look something like this:

We aren't going to talk about this type of chart in this book, because most people don't use them. Furthermore candlestick charts provide the same information, and they do it even better. Almost all day and swing traders rely on candlestick charts. An example is shown below.

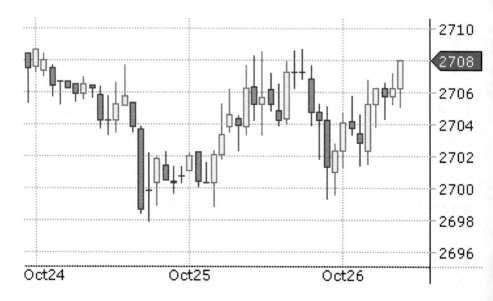

In chapter 4, we will discuss the candlestick charts in detail.

Clean Charts

Clean charts are simply charts that are free of indicators. You can have a line, bar, or candlestick chart that is a clean chart. With a clean chart, you will focus on price action and trending. In most cases, you will want to set your chart to use a weekly time frame for your bars or candlesticks. This will help you look at the chart and spot trends that are ongoing. A good practice to use with clean charts is to look at a years' worth of stock data and determine the price ranges that are currently being seen for the given stock. You will also want to analyze the charts to see if the recent price movements have broken out of previous price ranges, or whether they have narrowed their focus. You can also determine zones of support and resistance (see the following chapter).

Arithmetic Vs. Logarithmic Charts

Most charts in the financial world are used with logarithmic displays of pricing. You can also have simple arithmetic charts, which means that they are linear. On the x-axis, you are going to have a linear representation of time, and on the vertical or y-axis will be the pricing for the underlying security. Alternatively, you can set up your charts to show a logarithmic pricing scale. In this case, the differences in prices shown on the y-axis will be logarithmic and differ in terms of percentages. That is, the distance in ticks on the y-axis will be a certain percentage of the price, such as 5%. Technical traders prefer logarithmic charts. Using a logarithmic chart, it makes it easier to spot big price moves in terms of percentages, when the share price is relatively small. Think in terms of a chart showing prices from $0 to $500, and a price movement in the stock from $10 to $15. That would be hard to spot on a linear chart but easily displayed on a logarithmic chart.

In the next chapter, we are going to be looking at some basic chart patterns. These are rule-of-thumb approaches that have been used by traders for decades to determine when there are going to be trend reversals, and when to get into and out of stock trades.

Demo Accounts

Many readers are probably very excited about getting their feet wet with real trades. However, I am going to advise holding off. If you can find a broker that has a demo account feature, sign up for that first. A demo account lets you make simulated trades with the real market. That way, you can get some practice doing swing trading before you actually put money at risk. In any endeavor, gaining experience is a vital part of success. Everyone who is an expert at something practices first. Musicians practice and professional athletes practice as well. As a professional stock trader, you can practice too, and gain experience that will help you swing a trade for real while tipping the odds of success in your favor. Some people complain that the demo accounts have little value because the emotional component isn't there. In other words, you are going to be getting emotional when trading with real money on the line, and that might impact your judgment. That may very well be true. However, that doesn't mean that practicing isn't worth it. The point to practicing is that you can learn how to read charts, practice using technical indicators, and learn the best times to get in and out of trades.

Bullish Or Bearish?

Most readers have an intuitive sense of what these terms mean, but let's be precise with our language since we are educating ourselves on the art of swing trading. Bullish means that you believe the stock market is going to go up. We can also talk about bullish trades or bullish traders. If you are a bullish trader, this means that you are going to buy shares, looking for stock price appreciation in order to make profits.

Signals can be bullish or bearish too. A bullish chart pattern means that once the chart pattern completes, stock prices are expected to rise. They usually will, but not always. Indicators can give bullish signals, too. A bearish chart pattern or indicator means that a decline in stock prices is likely to follow. These are important signals to pay attention to, because the rise and fall of prices that follow a known pattern, signal, or indicator can be quite substantial. If you are not paying attention, you could face significant losses on your trades.

A bearish trader is one who foresees declining stock prices. In practice, a bearish trader will trade, hoping to make money from the dropping prices. This is done by shorting the stock.

Of course, these are ideal definitions. Nobody is always bullish or bearish. This is true, even if you never short a stock. Being bearish is, in part, a mood, so you may feel that stock prices are going to decline and avoid trading, so you are bearish even if you don't actually short the stock. As far as trading style, many traders are going to be bullish or bearish as the situation demands. Of course, there are extra requirements that have to be put in place so novice traders may not have the opportunity to act on bearish impulses. But experienced traders who are making a full-time living through swing trading or day trading may do so as the situation warrants.

Chapter 2: Making Sense Of Chart Patterns

As a stock trader, one of the most important things you need to learn is chart patterns that routinely show up on the stock market. These patterns form when trader behavior is changing, and momentum is shifting. This might indicate when interest in a given stock is increasing, and people are going to start buying up the stock in large numbers and pushing pricing up. Alternatively, prices might be at a peak, and the patterns might indicate that prices are going to start declining because a selloff is brewing. Meanwhile, you can use simple chart pattern analysis to spot a trend that you can capitalize on. These are simple rules of thumb, and although they are simple, many traders will get by through relying only on these techniques. Many fortunes were built doing so. However, since they were developed, more sophisticated tools will help you determine the best times to get in and out of trades and, therefore, help you more accurately forecast profits and losses.

Trading With The Trend

The first thing we are going to look at is trading with the trend. You want to get in on a trend at a relatively low price point if you see indications of an upward trend. The key to trading with the trend is to estimate where the trend is going. We do this by drawing trendlines. Most trading websites will allow you to put trendlines overlaid onto their stock charts so that you can make an estimate of where the trend is going. Then, you can pick a point to exit the trade. So the idea here is pretty simple, you buy now at a low price, and then you sell high later on down the trend. The slope of the trendline tells us where the trend is going to be in the future.

Keep in mind that you should not rely on any single tool described in this book. Obviously, things can happen that will cause a trend to stop in its tracks. Or a simple glance at a stock chart might make it seem like there is a trend when, in reality, the underlying data doesn't support the existence of a long-term trend. So as you develop your knowledge and skills about trading, you're going to want to use multiple tools together to make educated estimates of what stock prices are doing and where they are going to be in the future, and base your trades on that, rather than relying on any single tool by itself.

Creating Trendlines

The rule for trendlines when you are looking at increasing stock prices is simple. Stock prices are always fluctuating, and so there are going to be small dips in the stock price as it continues its upward march, assuming that we are in an uptrend. You start your trendline at the bottom of one of the troughs and then draw a straight line up, touching the bottoms of any dips in the chart. To be valid, it must touch a minimum of two troughs. Then, you just extend the line out the future, and you can get a pretty good estimate of where the stock price is going to be in the coming days or weeks. This will allow you to set up your trades since you can determine how much profit would be made buying shares of stock now and then selling them at a higher price level.

The example below from stockcharts.com shows just how to draw a trendline.

Notice that the trendline touches the low points of three dips, starting on December 22, 2008. The trendline estimated the price on March 23, 2009, would be $28 a share, but in fact, the trendline underestimated the price, since it actually moved higher, to $34 a share. Although it underestimated the price, that is not a big deal; it still showed us the general direction of stock prices. Had we bought shares at the beginning of the trend, we should have been able to sell them for a substantial profit. This is almost an ideal swing trade when it comes to trading with the trend.

Declining Trends And How To Short Stock

When stock prices are declining, you may wish to make a profit by shorting the stock. While investors are trapped by having to focus on only increasing stock prices, traders can make money either way. Shorting refers to selling something, while "long" refers to buying something to hold. Think long-term investment, although the term "long" is used by traders as well, as a kind of shorthand. So how do you profit by selling stocks?

The first step is you're going to need a margin account. This may not be something that everyone is interested in doing, and that's OK. As a trader, you can do just fine focusing on increasing stock prices, but if you are versatile and able to profit from shorting stocks as well, you're going to be better placed always to make profits. You'll be able to earn profits even during bear markets if you become acquainted with this method.

Let's see why we need a margin account and how it will enable us to earn a profit. Suppose that some stock is selling at $100 a share, and we think that it's going to crash after an "earnings call." In order to short the stock, the procedure is to borrow the shares from your broker. Thus, you need a margin account in order to use this strategy.

You borrow the shares, let's say that we borrow 100 shares. Then, you immediately sell them on the market. At $100 a share, 100 shares will go for $10,000. So we sell the shares, and $10,000 goes into our account. You've sold the stock, so you're short.

By the way, older treatments of stock trades worried about commissions, but so many brokerages are moving toward low or even zero commissions these days, we've decided to ignore commissions on trades for the purposes of this book. But when you open a brokerage account in order to begin stock trades, be sure to be aware of what commissions they are charging, if any.

OK, so you've got the $10,000. Let's suppose that the earnings call is bad and even worse than expected. Overnight and into the early morning trading, the stock price plummets. In an hour, it's down to $60 a share. Now you spring into action. Remember that you borrowed the shares from the broker, and so you need to settle your account by giving them back. Thankfully since you sold the shares you borrowed earlier at $100 a share, you have that $10,000 to play with. So you buy 100 shares back, at $60 a share, for a total of $6,000. Now you return the shares to the broker, and that makes them happy, and your account is free and clear. And since you only had to spend $6,000 to get the shares back, you've made a $4,000 profit.

Not bad for a day's work.

That is how to short a stock in a nutshell. So an earnings call is a dramatic example, but quite often there are just declining price trends. Learning how to spot them can be important if you want to have this technique in your repertoire.

When looking at downward trends, this time, we draw our trendline on the peaks of the trend. Then, you draw it with a downward slope, assuming that prices are declining. This graphic below shows an upward trendline and a downward trendline on the same chart so that you can be familiar with how both are properly drawn.

Since we are drawing trendlines that are upward using the troughs, and downward trendlines using the peaks, we are likely to underestimate rising prices and overestimate falling prices. That is a good position to be in; you want to take a conservative approach in making your estimates.

So if a stock is trading at $50 a share, and your trendline shows that it's going to reach $65 a share in a week since it's likely to go higher, you've made a safer and more conservative estimate of your possible profit. You can make a trade and put in a sell order if the shares get to $65 that will automatically execute. Since the real trend may end up stronger, this increases the odds that your trade is going to come out successful. The stock may actually reach $70 a share, but as a swing trader, you want to be conservative, not greedy. If you get greedy, more often than not, you are going to find yourself staying in your trades too long, and then prices are going to reverse and wipe out your positions.

The Poor Man's Short

Not everyone is going to open a margin account and have the capacity to borrow large numbers of shares. However, there is a backdoor way that virtually any trader can use to short stocks. This is done using exchange-traded funds.

Exchange-traded funds are mutual funds that trade live on the stock exchange. It is not our purpose here to discuss the details and nuances of exchange-traded funds versus mutual funds, but just be aware that there are many exchange-traded funds on the market that work exactly like stocks. You buy shares of them on the market, and you can sell the shares on the market. This is done without the involvement or intervention of a financial manager. Moreover, mutual funds only trade after a market close.

There are exchange-traded funds for virtually anything. For example, many track major market indexes, so you can invest in SPY to track the S & P 500, or DIA to track the Dow Jones Industrial Average.

Lesser known is the exchange-traded funds that short the market. So basically, this is a fund that shorts the market for you, so that you don't have to. Keep in mind that these types of funds are not for specific stocks, so you aren't going to be able to use this tool to short the likes of Apple and Facebook. However, if the entire market is dropping, you can use the funds to short the market.

Using the funds in this way is simple. They gain value when the major indexes are losing value. During a recession, they can gain very large amounts of value, perhaps rising 10x in price or more.

So when the stock market is declining in price, you can use these types of funds for a swing trade. You simply buy to enter a position when the stock market begins declining. Then, when you believe it has reached maximum decline or you have reached a profit level that you find acceptable, you sell your shares. So it's a long position – but a long position in an asset that moves inversely to the overall market.

This is just a method to keep in mind. You can also purchase shares of these funds when times are good, as a type of insurance that you just hold onto. During bull markets, these funds are low cost on a per-share basis. So you can load up on some shares, and just hold them until there is a market crash. While it's been a long time since there has been a major downturn on the stock market, one thing you can always count on is one is coming. As you are now aware of this, don't be left behind next time.

Trendlines: Time Horizons

The time horizon used for your trendline is going to be important. Trends that occur over short time horizons may disappear when looking at longer time horizons. So what is important? That depends on the time horizon of your trade. If you are a day trader, then you are going to be wanting to look at trendlines over 15-minute to hourly time frames. For swing traders, there are many different approaches, since there is wide latitude in how long swing traders are going to stay in a trade. If you are going to be trading for more than two weeks, then a weekly chart is going to be the most useful for drawing your trendlines, but any swing trader can use daily charts as well.

Trendlines: The Kickback

When drawing trendlines, watch out for reversals.

Trendlines: 3 Questions

Trendlines are important to use in your analysis as a swing trader, and they are not all that complicated to understand and use.

Why Are Trendlines Important?

Trendlines show the direction of stock prices and where they are likely to end up at a future date. A swing trader wants to trade the swing in stock prices, and a trendline helps the swing trader determine when to enter and exit trades, and what pricing level is going to be important for exiting the trade. That will also help you determine the profit level of your trade that is realistically possible.

What Do You Do When A Trendline Is Broken?

When a trendline is broken, meaning the price is either stagnating or moving in the opposite direction, wait for a retest. A retest occurs when the price returns to the trendline. If you are looking to get into a trade, wait for the candlesticks to touch the trendline again.

What Is a Breakout?

A breakout occurs when the stock rises above or below long-standing boundaries of stock prices. When you spot a breakout, you can draw trendlines to make estimates of take-profit levels for a trade to take advantage of the new price movement.

Support And Resistance

Earlier, we mentioned that stocks often get trapped in a zone of prices, and the stock price stays within a given range, going up to a certain price level and then dropping down to a certain price level.

The upper price level that the stock can't seem to break above is called the *resistance*. The lower bounding price level is called *support*. The trading idea here is pretty simple. First, you need to see the price of the stock drop down and touch the support price level, which you can draw as a straight line across the chart, at least twice before you consider making the trade. You also want to see the stock price rise up to the resistance price level at least twice, but without breaking above it.

Now, if you are looking to profit from increasing stock prices, you wait for the stock to drop back down to the support level. At this point, you have to be using all of your stock trading analysis tools and be keenly aware of any signs that the stock is going to drop out and begin declining below the support price level. If those signs are not there, then you buy your shares at the support price, and then you want to sell them just before the price rises up enough to reach the resistance price.

This chart of Halliburton stock from stockcharts.com illustrates this concept. Notice that, in this case, the stock was ranging between support and resistance from October all the way through April. So there were a lot of opportunities for patient swing traders to earn profits from this stock utilizing this method. The support level was $33 a share, and the resistance level was nearly $43 a share, so you had several opportunities to make nearly $10 a share in profit.

This method can be used for shorting stocks as well. In that case, you borrow shares when they are priced at the higher, resistance level price. Then, you just wait for them to drop back down to the support pricing level, and buy them back to book your profits.

Of course, there are going to be times when the stock is going to break out of this pattern. This is either going to happen when the stock crashes through the support level to start a downward trend, or if it breaks above the resistance price level to begin an upward trend. In order to assess when that might be a possibility, you will have to learn how to use candlestick charts and moving averages, which we will talk about later in the book.

The Megaphone Pattern

The next pattern that we are going to look at is kind of like ranging, but as time goes on, the stock reaches higher highs and lower lows. As such, the stock prices form a broadening pattern as time advances, forming a megaphone shape.

To find the megaphone pattern, you draw two trendlines at the same time-period on the chart, an upward-pointing trendline, and a downward pointing trendline. This will estimate the lows and high prices of the stock in the near future, and help you trade on the swings.

Classic 'megaphone'

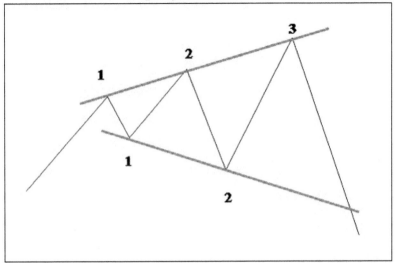

Source: Janney Capital Markets

In the chart above, imagine that we have not yet reached point 3 on the chart, but instead have just passed the low at point 2. In that case, we would have enough information to determine that the stock was in the megaphone pattern, and therefore we can extend out the trendlines to estimate where points 3 will be. If we are interested in buying the stock at a low price, when the stock has just passed point 2 of the low, we can buy shares. Then, knowing that the stock is in the megaphone pattern, we are well-positioned to hold the stock until it rises to a price near point 3, which we estimate from drawing the upward trendline. At this point, we sell the shares and book our profits.

On the other hand, if you were looking to short the stock, you'd simply wait until the stock reached point 3, and then borrow shares from the broker and sell them. Then, we use the trendline to make an estimate of where we should buy the shares back at the lower price so we can return the shares to the broker and take our profits.

Head And Shoulders

The head and shoulders pattern is the first pattern we are going to encounter that will help us determine that the momentum of a trend has fizzled out. A "head and shoulders" pattern will occur at the end of an upward trend in prices. It will have a left shoulder, which is an early peak in prices, that drops back down again to a level called the neckline. Then, the head will form as buying pressure resumes, and prices are pushed to an even higher level. But now we see the key point in the formation of the head and shoulders pattern – the momentum isn't there to push prices higher, and so they drop back down to the neckline again. At this point, you can be reasonably convinced that momentum in this upward trend has run out. But if you want to wait, look for the formation of a second shoulder, the right shoulder, where prices rise up again, but only about as high as they did in the first shoulder. Then, they drop down to the neckline again, and you can be reasonably assured that this is going to be the start of a downward trend in prices, in most cases. This is illustrated below in the chart from Wikipedia by Altaf Qadir.

One of the advantages of the head and shoulders chart pattern is that it will appear on all time frames if the conditions are right, and this makes it useful for swing traders that are trading with any time horizon. Furthermore, your conditions for exiting a position are well spelled out. Notice that the neckline price is reached 4 times. By the time it's appeared 3 times, you can place a limit order to sell at the neckline price. That way, if the pattern continues, you'll be out of your position before the stock begins declining without recovery. However, if the pattern fails to form, your limit order won't execute, and you can take advantage of more rising prices if the stock breaks to the upside.

Keep in mind that in the real world, a chart formation like this is not always going to display in a pure academic format, because of the inherent noise in the system. Sometimes, the head won't rise above the shoulders, but the general shape of the pattern, three peaks, is there. So don't look for perfection when you are looking for a head and shoulders pattern in real data. As this example shows, the pattern may not be quite symmetrical, and you will see some retracements mixed in with the data. Notice that the neckline isn't exactly straight all the time in real-world data either, although it will be relatively close. In the example below, there is some noisy data in the formation of the head, and the right shoulder isn't a perfect formation either.

GAIA - Gaiam Inc - Daily Candlestick Chart

Op:12.99, Hi:13.42, Lo:12.83, Cl:13.21   ■ EXPMA (20): 14.04   □ EXPMA (50): 15.28   ■ EXPMA (200): 18.34

Left Shoulder   Head

Right Shoulder

Neckline

Classic Head and Shoulders Reversal Pattern

Vol: 275,700

Flip this over and the upside-down head and shoulders, where prices decline but then return to the neckline by rising back up, is an indication that a downward trend in prices has come to an end. This is called an inverse head and shoulders. The left shoulder of an inverse head and shoulders is going to start with declining prices that move below the neckline price. It will decline to a certain level and then retrace to the neckline. Then, it will decline again to an even lower price level, forming the head. The price then reverts back to the neckline. Finally, it will move back to a lower price that is close to the price reached in the left shoulder, forming a right shoulder as it again reverts to the neckline. The inverse head and shoulders pattern usually means that there is going to be a breakout to the upside.

As we will demonstrate below in "Failed Patterns," you can get tricked by a head and shoulders formation. Although a head and shoulders formation usually means that prices are going to enter a downtrend, sometimes they will break to the upside. The same is true for an inverse head and shoulders, where prices can actually break to the downside after it forms. The biggest mistake that a trader can make is making a move too soon. At the very least, you need to let the pattern form before exiting a position or entering a position if you are looking at an inverse head and shoulders.

Some more conservative traders will place a stop-loss limit order at the peak price of the left shoulder. However, I recommend using the neckline, in case there is a break to the upside as the formation is nearing completion. The hidden assumption here is that you have entered your position at a much lower price, and the head and shoulders pattern is appearing after an uptrend.

The head and shoulders pattern occurs because prices have been pushed up beyond inherent value by latecomers to a stock rally. After they push prices up to the head, there aren't any more takers for the stock, and some begin selling off. However, some traders who are not careful about these matters are still going to have the psychological pull of having seen the price going high, entice them into buying, so there is a final rally that generates the right shoulder, pushing up prices once again. But this time, the market truly runs out of steam, and people begin selling off to avoid huge losses.

But as always, many things can impact the stock price, and unexpected events can cause a breakout trend in a different direction. Also, with the chaotic nature of stock data, people (especially novice traders) will see patterns that really aren't there in the data. The best thing to do if you are new to trading is to study past examples from real data of the head and shoulders pattern. Also, keep some awareness in your mind that these patterns work most of the time, but not all of the time. This means that you should use multiple tools to confirm your trades.

Double Top Pattern

The double top stock pattern is another familiar chart pattern that indicates an upward trend in stock prices is running out of momentum. Simply put, these types of patterns tell us that at the higher pricing levels, it's getting harder and harder to find more bullish investors, and the stock has reached a point where it's overpriced. Some latecomers will buy some shares, temporarily pushing prices up a little, but then prices are going to drop off as people actually beginning selling off their overpriced shares. This happens when large numbers of traders start to recognize that they better get out before they lose their opportunity for profit.

In the chart below by Altaf Qadir, we see the double top pattern. Like the head and shoulders pattern, we are going to see the stock rising to a peak and then repeatedly hitting a low point, going up to a peak, and then finally breaking out to the downside. The key to this pattern is that there are two high peaks in prices, forming the double top pattern, but you see stock prices rise to the peak, and then fall back down because of a lack of momentum.

Sometimes, stock prices can appear to be running out of steam, only to resume the upward trend. This *could* happen after the stock reaches the first tip, but the signal that this is a double top and that it's actually best to get out of the stock is when the second peak is reached, and stock prices begin falling. At that point, when they reach the "neckline" to borrow the terminology from the head and shoulders, or the point where you see two dips to local low points, then it's probably time to sell your shares before the downward trend in prices gains momentum.

Like the head and shoulders, flip the pattern over, and it can occur at the bottom of a downward trend, indicating a reversal into upward trending prices.

The Rounded Top

The rounded top is another typical chart pattern that indicates stock prices are going to start dropping off. Once again, it's a signal that momentum in buying pressure has run out, and investors are starting to get cold feet on the stock, and they begin selling off. A rounded top is a long-term trend pattern that will take weeks or even months to form. It is basically an upside-down u-shape at the peak of a stock uptrend or a bowl shape at the bottom of a downward trend that indicates buyers are getting back in the stock, and this will start an uptrend.

A rounded top is divided into a set of sequences, with five stages in total. In the first stage, we have the long-term uptrend that the stock has already been in for some time. This is followed by the first leg, which is a continuation of the upward trend, but it starts rounding off to a peak. The start of the first leg forms the neckline. The next stage is the tipping point, where stocks rise to a peak and start dropping. This can be more sudden and short term, forming a V-shape, or it can be slow and gradual, forming an upside-down bowl at the top of the pricing trend. Now the stock enters the second leg, where stock prices begin to steadily drop, going back to the price level where the first leg started. At this point, if you have been long on the stock, it is a good time to sell your shares and get out of the trade. This is because the stock is about to enter into the final stage, called breakout, where the downward trend begins. At the neckline, it's a definite sell.

The example below is actually from Forex using the MetaTrader 4 software, but the principles are exactly the same.

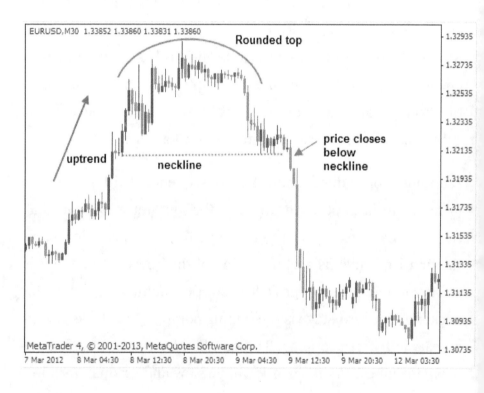

Cup And Handle

A cup and handle chart pattern is a bullish formation on a stock chart. It is more important for longer trades that last at least three weeks and possibly up to six months. The formation begins with a price drop, which then rises to form the "cup" pattern. During the formation of the cup pattern, the price will drop slightly and then rise again on the right side. The cup part of the pattern should show a shallow, rounded drop. After the cup has formed, there will be a sharp drop that does not dip as low as the cup portion of the pattern, and this will be followed by a break to the upside. This is illustrated as shown below:

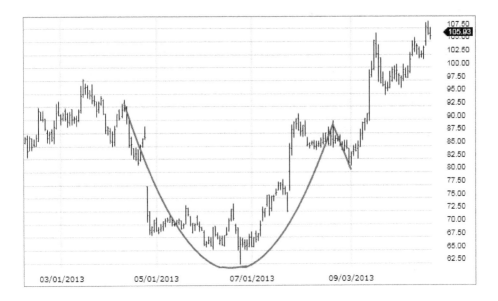

This chart illustrates some of the pitfalls in looking for chart patterns to trade, since a perfectly round "cup" is not formed, due to the noise or price fluctuations that always occur in the midst of stock market data. So you will be looking for an approximate shape, not the exact shape that you are going to see in textbooks. Again, using candlestick charts is something that is going to help you determine what is real and what isn't, and when making a trade is a good move.

With the cup and handle, you are looking to enter a trade to take advantage of upside gains. Wait for the pattern to form completely, and then trade at the far right portion of the pattern, which is the handle.

Pennants And Flags

A pennant is known as a consolidation pattern. This means that for a time, the stock price is trapped in a narrow range of values. The pennant begins with a steep rise in value. Think of a flag hovering on a pole, so the stock price should shoot up, and then consolidate. With a pennant, the consolidation period will narrow or converge, giving the shape of a pennant that narrows toward the end. A flag will simply range between two values. The ranging or consolidation period can last 1-3 weeks. The consolidation period is then followed by a large breakout to the upside, and so this is considered a bullish pattern.

The steep rise in price can happen quickly or over a period of time. In the first chart shown below, we see a steep rise in price, followed by the continuation pattern which narrows, and then a break to the upside.

In this example, there is a more extended rise in price, so there is not a literal "flagpole."

Flag patterns are similar but show less convergence during the consolidation period. You can also have inverse pennants and flags. In that case, there is a steep decline in price, followed by a period of consolidation, and a break toward the downside.

Triple Top And Triple Bottom

A triple top or a triple bottom is somewhat similar to a head and shoulders or inverse head and shoulders pattern. Look for this type of pattern to form after there has been a long-term trend. For a triple top, there would be a long-term trend in increasing prices. For a triple bottom, you look for a long-term trend in decreasing prices.

Let's consider a triple top first. In this case, the upward trend continues, but it reaches a peak and then declines to a relatively low price, then rebounds to increase again. Unlike the head and shoulders, in the second peak, it rises to a price that is equal to the first peak price that was reached, and before going higher, the price declines again to the same low price. It will then reverse and rise again, reaching the same matching price, before dropping again, at which point it will break to the downside.

As we discussed with the head and shoulders and cup and handle, in the real world, patterns are rarely academic in form. So you should look for approximations of this pattern rather than seeking an exact match. Second, if you are going to trade on patterns (all swing traders should be aware of patterns, regardless of whether or not you are using them as your primary tool), you need to wait for the pattern to form completely, before making major decisions on your trades.

The triple bottom is just a flipped-over version of the triple top. Hence, in this case, the price is going to decrease for a time, reaching the low point, then the price will bounce back to a neckline price, drop again to the low point, return to the neckline, drop again, and then increase and break to the upside.

If you see a triple bottom form after a declining price trend, it is a bullish buy signal. A triple top after an uptrend in prices is a bearish signal, which means you should sell shares.

Falling Wedge Or Symmetric Triangle

A falling wedge is a pattern that is somewhat similar to a pennant formation. In this case, you are not necessarily going to see a flagpole in the pattern. The pattern should be set up by an uptrend in prices, even though there won't be a rise in prices as steep as seen with a flagpole. However, you are going to see a period of time that includes a pattern that can be described as somewhat consolidating, but gradually declining. Think of it like a pennant pattern that is tipped down somewhat. In order to find this pattern, to confirm it, if you suspect it is forming, use the following technique. Draw two trendlines, one on the top of the pattern that touches the peak prices for the time period, and a second trendline on the bottom of the pattern that touches the low prices for the time period. What you are looking for is the two trendlines to converge. At the point of convergence, or just before it, you should see a sign of a coming break to the upside in the form of increased prices that break above the upper trendline.

If the trendlines actually meet, you have a balanced triangle. If they don't exactly meet, then you have a falling wedge pattern.

When the trendlines converge, showing that you have a falling wedge pattern, this indicates that a breakout to the upside is likely to occur. Be sure to confirm with other tools or technical indicators, but a falling wedge is a good bullish or buy signal in most cases.

Patterns Gone Wrong

It is easy for novice traders to get caught up by patterns that go wrong. Remember that the stock market is chaotic by nature, and so you should expect that sometimes when patterns appear to be forming, a price movement in an unexpected direction can occur. The way to avoid being trapped by this kind of situation is to never rely on a single pattern or indicator during your trading. Use multiple tools in order to make the best judgments. You also should have some awareness of the fact that you are not going to be able to win on every single trade, no matter how much analysis you perform.

Failed Patterns

It's easy, even for experienced traders, to be tricked by patterns that appear to be forming, but really don't. We are presenting the patterns above after they have completed, when you are actually trading, and the patterns are in formation, it can be difficult to really be absolutely sure about what you are seeing.

There are some special cases of failed patterns. In some cases, momentum will suddenly reverse, after a pattern indicating a shift is happening, has formed. Any reason can lead to this, remember that the stock market is chaotic, and the news is always hitting the airwaves that can cause a sudden pricing shift.

There are a couple of special cases to be aware of. However, these are called traps.

Many times, patterns will appear to form perfectly on the charts but fail to produce the expected results, or they will be forming well but fail to form as the pattern comes to a close completely. To help avoid falling for these errors, you will need to employ other tools in your analysis. One of the most useful is candlestick charts, which are discussed in chapter 4, as they will give you more clues to rely on in order to determine how the stock price is really going to move.

In this example, we see a failed head and shoulder chart. The pattern formed, but then the stock broke to the upside:

The clue is with the weak shoulder formations, most importantly on the left shoulder. Notice that there is not much of a peak on the left shoulder, and later, when we learn about candlesticks, the large white candlestick that pushes the price up is the main piece of data that indicates a break to the upside.

Bear Traps

A bear trap is a chart pattern that incorrectly signals a coming downtrend in prices. These signals are called traps because they

59

can entice investors into making the wrong decisions. Especially if you are a novice trader, you can end up selling your shares prematurely in a bear trap.

A bear trap can occur when investors incorrectly see a signal of declining prices, and so bearish investors (those hoping for or seeing stock price declines) short the stock, driving down prices temporarily (from a lot of people selling off). The trap is set, and it looks like a downtrend is starting, and this might entice more bearish investors to short the stock. Panicked long investors might sell their shares also, exiting their trades too early and putting some downward pressure on the price. But in the case of the trap, they incorrectly interpreted the signals in the chart, and prices start reversing, resuming the upward trend.

Bull Trap

A bull trap occurs in the midst of a downturn. In the case of a bull trap, traders will see signals of price increases in the data, and they will start buying up shares. This will lead to a small bump in prices, as those falling for the trap push prices up a little bit. And that in itself might entice more investors to buy shares. The trap forms when the overall downward pricing momentum is still stronger than the momentum caused by the bullish investors that misinterpreted the data, and so the upward march in prices is temporary and not very strong, and downward trends resume.

How To Know When You're In A Trap

You can't really know when you are in a trap, but the best way to avoid it is to use several signals and technical indicators together, rather than relying only on one chart pattern or tool. When multiple indicators agree, this is a sign that a changing price trend is real. If you see an indicator of a changing price trend or a particular chart pattern, but it's not confirmed by other data or indicators, that is a strong sign that it's a trap.

Setting Price Targets

Use trendlines to set your price target. The price target should be a reasonable estimate of when to get out of a trade and make a reasonable profit. Don't expect or wait around for huge profits on a single trade. If you make $5 a share on a trade, you've done quite well for a single trade. Sometimes, trends will be very strong, and this should show up in your trendlines. In that case, draw the trendline out a reasonable distance, and then set the price level for take-profit to exit your trades.

Some Tips For The Successful Use Of Patterns

As a swing trader, knowing your patterns and using them to help you determine when to enter and exit trades is important. The first thing to keep in mind with patterns is that you shouldn't overuse them. Don't rely on patterns alone. In the modern market, there are many tools that a trader has access to that can help them determine when to enter and exit trades. You should use at a minimum three tools together and make your trades when they all agree on what is going on. Patterns are right most of the time, but they are not always right, and it's also easy to get fooled into seeing patterns on stock charts that aren't really there. In a sense, a stock chart can be a type of Rorschach test, where people can, at times, see what they want to see. To be sure that a pattern is really there when you think it's forming, wait for it to form before making a trading decision completely.

A second thing that you need to keep in mind when trading based on chart patterns is that you should always use trendlines. Trendlines are always useful when trading on patterns. Although you are only going to have one trendline with a head and shoulders formation, for example, you are still going to have one that represents the neckline. It may be straight or not, but it should be close to straight as judged by anyone using reasonable criteria.

Also, be sure to be familiar with the behavior of stock prices in the time leading up to the appearance of a pattern. If a pattern is known to form after an uptrend in prices, such as a falling wedge, you need to keep that in mind, not just look for the wedge pattern. The behavior of stock prices before the pattern forms is just as important as the pattern itself.

Finally, as we have been emphasizing, patterns are not the be-all and end-all of stock trading. They are one tool among many. We are going to discuss all of the most frequently used tools in swing trading in this book, and you should become familiar with all of them, and use them in conjunction with patterns. Some traders who are gifted with intuition on the stock market are able to do quite well-using pattern trading, but most of us should incorporate tools like moving averages together with pattern trading to make our decisions.

So for example, if you are seeing a pattern like a falling wedge that would indicate a break to the upside, if a trend reversal to the upside is also indicated with moving averages (we will discuss this in chapter 5), then you can be reasonably confident that this is a good time to be bullish. This is a better approach than going on the pattern alone, which can fail. However, when a pattern fails, while there are not necessarily going to be some signs in the pattern itself, there are going to be other clues that the pattern is going to fail that you are going to spot using other tools and indicators.

Chapter 3: The Bread-And-Butter Chart Patterns To Afford Caviar-And-Blini Dinners

In this chapter, we are going to get into some more complex stock chart patterns that are known as ABCD chart patterns. These are chart patterns based on Gartley patterns that were described by a stock trader named H.M. Gartley in the mid-1930s. They have proven to be indispensable tools for swing traders, and they help you identify market swings in the making and estimate the enter and exit prices for a trade.

Gartley Patterns

In 1935, H.M. Gartley published his findings in a book called Profits in the Stock Market, which laid out harmonic patterns that regularly occur in stock market charts. Gartley studied swing moves and explained how to use them in order to make profits on the stock market. Gartley patterns are reputed to have a 70% success rate in picking winning trades.

In order to understand Gartley and ABCD patterns, you need to understand the concept of retracement. Retracement is simply a reversal in the price of a stock that is temporary. Remember that stock prices are volatile, or somewhat chaotic. During an upward trend in prices, due to the chaotic nature of stock trading, the price is not going to go up along a smooth curve. Instead, the price will periodically decrease, while the overall upward trend continues. The price will retrace back to a previous lower price, before rising again and resuming the upward trend.

There are two general types of Gartley patterns. They can be Bearish or Bullish. A Bearish Gartley pattern is a sell indicator. A Bullish Gartley pattern is a buy indicator. The patterns are labeled by points ABCD on a stock market chart and will show retracements. There are many different Gartley Patterns, and you can spend some in-depth time studying them in detail.

Gartley patterns are said to be harmonic, for those who are mathematically inclined. While modern Gartley patterns are based on Fibonacci numbers, Gartley didn't specifically reference that, and only focused on the ratios. Each Gartley patter will have a stop-loss point that is identified as Point 0 or X, and a take-profit point that is identified at point C.

Stop-Loss Levels

As a swing trader, you should always set what is known as a stop-loss level on your trades. When you place a stock trade, you can enter what is called a limit order. The limit order is an order that will only execute if a limit price specified in the order is reached. Hence, for example, if a stock is trading at $200 a share, a trader might be willing to take a $4 loss per share on the trade, but no more than that. So they can make this automatic by placing a limit order to sell the stock automatically if the share price drops to $196. That is a stop-loss such that the trader won't be stuck with the shares if the price continues dropping below $196 a share.

Take-Profit Levels

A take-profit level is another type of limit order that you can place with many brokers. So this is an automatic sell level if the stock price rises to a certain level. The reason to place take-profit orders is so that you don't get overwhelmed by euphoria when stock prices are rising and make bad decisions in the process. When stock prices are rising, traders can get greedy and start imagining themselves, making large amounts of money. In the midst of their greed, they will stay in trades too long and ignore the signs that a downward trend is forming, as they hope for more and more profits. Then, they get caught with their pants down as the stock price suddenly plummets, and often they end up making very small profits or even no profits at all.

If you set a take-profit level in a limit order, you are freed from having to monitor the stock constantly, and you are assured of making a certain level of profits. You can determine ahead of each trade the amount of profit that you want to make and set your take-profit limit order accordingly. The amount you want to earn in a trade can be done by studying resistance and support levels and trendlines, for example.

Bullish ABCD Pattern

There are many different ABCD patterns, and we remind the reader that you should devote time to learning them independently, as a thorough knowledge of ABCD patterns is something that requires a bit of study all its own. If you are going to be a swing trader, understanding ABCD patterns is going to be important for your success.

A bullish ABCD pattern is going to see the stock start at price level X, rise up to price level A, and then retrace to a lower price B, which is going to be higher than price level X. Then, it will rise again to price level C, which is going to be lower than price level A. Then, it is going to drop to a new low D, which is lower than B, but higher than X. If the ratios that are seen are correct, the point D is taken to be a BUY signal. Following D, the prediction is that after retracements to price B and price D, the stock price will now rise higher than price A. The overall layout of the chart and ratios is shown below.

Bullish Gartley

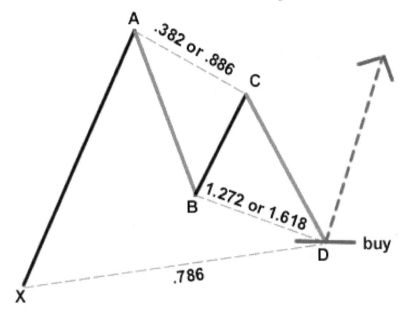

To do the analysis, the first thing you want to note is the magnitude in the price difference between point A and point X. Then, you will compare the magnitude of the retracement to point B to this amount. It should be 61.8% of the line XA. Of course, in practice, it does not have to be exact, but the closer it is to this value, the better the pattern that is forming.

Now, you look at BC and compare that to the line AB. Here, you expect BC to be in the range of 38.2% to 88.6% of the length of AB. Then, the CD can be 1.272% to 1.618% of AB. Finally, the CD should be a retracement of up to 78.6% of XA. The point D is called the potential reversal zone. Point D is a buy signal, and you will probably set A or C as your take-profit level. If you place a stop-loss order, you will use X.

Bearish ABCD Pattern

The Bearish ABCD pattern is basically the same, but with the positions of all the points altered by flipping the pattern over. So we start at a high price X, which then drops to a low price A. Then, there is a retracement to B, as this time, we are in a trend of declining stock prices. The stock price will then drop back down to C, but it won't be quite as low in price as A. From here, the price will rise again to point D, which is the sell signal. The proportions are the same as used with the bullish Gartley pattern. Remember that the values given do not have to be exact, but the closer they are, the better.

Below is an illustration of the bearish pattern.

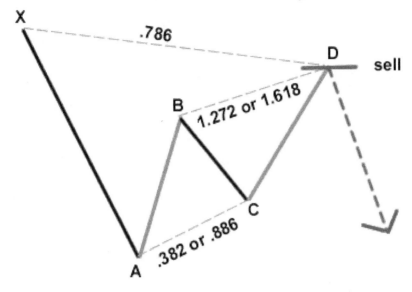

Bearish Gartley

Time Horizons

It is important to look at stock charts on different time frames. Different time frames can reveal different trends in the pricing data. On a monthly interval, the stock price might be rising. But on a weekly time frame, it could be dropping. Meanwhile, it might rise on a given day. As a swing trader, you should look at the charts using different time horizons in order to see how the overall trends are going and what trends exist inside the overall trend, depending on what time frame you are using for your swing trades. For example, if you are looking to make weekly trades, then the weekly trend is going to be your main focus, and then you will look at the cycles and trends within the weekly trend, looking at daily and even hourly time horizons.

Retracements Versus Reversals

In doing your analysis, it is going to be important to distinguish between retracements and reversals. In the heat of the moment, it is going to be hard to do so, and you are going to be wondering if a downturn in stock price is just a blip in the chaos of the market, or if it is the start of a real price reversal that would wipe out your trade if you don't sell at the right time.

Remember that a retracement is a temporary reversal in price, and it occurs in the middle of a larger trend. A trend in the upward direction is indicated by a series of higher high prices. It is going to have lows in its midst as well, but the lows are going to be higher lows as time moves on, so even the lows are contributing to the upward trend. In contrast, a trend in the downward direction is indicated by lower lows in succession. Also, like an uptrend, a downtrend is going to have lower highs in its midst.

To look for a reversal in an uptrend, you will seek a lower low and a lower high.

So during an uptrend, you might see the price go in the following sequence: $50, $52, $51, $52, $54, $55, $53, $54, $56, $57. Notice that the lows in the sequence are $50, $51, $53. So the lows are higher lows, we don't just have higher highs in the uptrend. If the sequence went to $55, $53, $56 after having peaked at $57, now we see lower lows and lower highs, indicating a price reversal.

The time frame of a price movement obviously distinguishes a reversal from a retracement. A retracement is going to last for a relatively short time period. It is a temporary price reversal that will quickly end, and the main trend will resume.

In a retracement, although there is a temporary drop in stock price, the larger trend continues. There are still going to be higher lows and higher highs in a retracement (for an upward trend – just reverse everything to understand how things will work in a downtrend).

Trend Identification

To summarize, to identify an upward trend, look for a sequence of higher high prices and higher lows as time moves forward. The longer you can see this sequence, especially if it quickly resumes after a retracement, the more confidence you have in the trend.

For a downward trend in prices, you will do the reverse. So a downward trend can be identified with a sequence of lower high prices and lower low prices as time goes on. The longer the trend continues, the more confidence that you can have that the trend is real.

When you establish that a trend has been identified, then you can draw trendlines to estimate where the trend is going to end up at some specific point in the future. As a swing trader, you can be rigid in your approach, and pick a specific time or price level where you want to exit your trade, or you can take a relaxed approach and handle it manually. Only do the latter if you are confident in your capacity to avoid getting wrapped up emotionally in your trades.

Avoid Getting Emotional

We have already mentioned one way that can happen, and that is when you are getting greedy and looking for more profits than you should be realistically aiming for, and so in the midst of your euphoria, you stay in your trades too long.

Of course, the other way that emotions can mix up your trades is panic. There is always going to be the fear that you are going to lose all of your money that is riding on a trade. No matter how irrational this fear is, it will be there when real money is on the line, especially when we are talking about entering into trades of thousands of dollars at a time. That is why setting stop-loss orders is important. Use a set-it and forget-it method of putting your stop-loss order that will automatically get you out of the trade, and just accept it once you've placed the order. Sometimes, you are going to be getting out of trades prematurely, but more often than not, you are going to be preventing yourself from taking more losses than you should be taking.

Using the 2% Rule

A good rule of thumb recommended by financial advisors is that you only risk 2% of your account on any trade. This defines the amount of loss that you are willing to accept. So if you are trading 50 shares of a stock with a share price of $100, and you have $10,000 in your account, to find the stop-loss point you calculate 2% of your account size, which in this case is $200. Divide by the number of shares in the trade to determine the amount of loss you can accept. In this example, it gives us a loss of $4 a share. That means that we can set a stop-loss order for $96, so if the stock drops to $96 a share our holdings will automatically sell, protecting us against further losses.

Bottom Line Of Chart Patterns

In the past two chapters, we've examined some of the most important chart patterns used by swing traders. This is an introductory book, and you should explore this further and learn them all. Some traders who are better at the "art" of trading, are very well placed to rely on chart patterns to make profits. However, most of us would be foolish to only rely on chart patterns in order to make profitable trades. This is even more true for beginners. You get a sense of chart patterns as you gain experience trading. As a beginner, you should rely more on hard data to make your trading decisions. You can use hard data in conjunction with the chart patterns. So when you recognize a chart pattern, compare it to what the candlestick charts and technical indicators are telling you. When everything agrees, then make your move.

Chapter 4: The Nuts And Bolts Of Candlestick Charts

In this chapter, we turn to one of the most important tools used by swing traders—the candlestick chart. A candlestick chart divides up stock market data into trading sessions that can be of varying lengths. They can be as short as 1 minute or a full day or longer. The time frame used to define a trading session is up to you, and it will depend on your trading style and goals. For example, day traders are likely to use 5-minute time intervals. If you are looking to trade on the scale of days, you might use 1-hour or 4-hour time intervals. A swing trader looking for profits over the course of weeks may use daily time intervals.

What Candlesticks Show

Candlesticks show the pricing action for each time frame. The color of a candlestick is used to indicate whether the price rose or fell in the trading session. If the price rises, it's a bullish candlestick, and on most stock charts, this is indicated with the color green. If the chart has a black background, it will either be a green outline or a white outline. On black and white charts (which aren't used nearly as much anymore), a bullish candlestick is indicated by a black outline, and so will be white in the middle.

A bearish candlestick indicates that the price fell during the trading session. In this case, they are usually colored red. However, on some charts with a black background, they may actually be colored solid white. On a black and white chart, they will be colored solid black.

Most charts used for trading stocks are presented with a white background, so look for green colored candlesticks in the bullish case, and red candlesticks for the bearish case. You may be able to set your own coloring options depending on the website or broker that you are using.

Each candlestick is going to have a wick or shadow sticking out of the top and bottom of the candlestick, which is actually referred to as the body. The wick that sticks out of the top of the body represents the high price of the trading session. So you will always be interested to see how high prices were pushed up during a trading session, and how that compares to the opening and closing prices.

The bottom wick of a candlestick represents the low price for a trading session. This is another piece of data that you will want to compare to the opening and closing prices of the trading session. If the wick is long, that indicates that the price dropped well below the opening and closing prices of the trading session, but the price got pushed up by the close of the trading session.

That indicates that there was a lot of selling activity at some point during the trading session, but then bullish investors were able to push prices back up to a higher level. This could indicate that there is a trend brewing in the bullish direction.

Likewise, a long wick on the top indicates that prices were pushed up high during the trading session, but it ran out of momentum. A long wick on the top as compared to the body indicates that bearish investors sold off enough shares to push prices back down again by the session close, meaning that there might be a bearish situation developing.

The top and bottom of the candlestick body have a specific meaning, depending on the color of the candlestick. If the candlestick is green or bullish, the bottom of the candlestick is the opening price for the trading session, and the top of the candlestick is the closing price for the trading session. On red or bearish candlesticks, the top of the body represents the opening price, and the bottom of the body represents the closing price. Since the bottom is a lower price level than the top, this reflects the fact that the share price dropped during the closing session. The basic structure of candlesticks is illustrated below (images created by Probe-meteo.com, from Wikipedia).

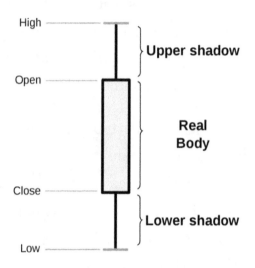

High — Upper shadow

Open —

Real Body

Close —

Lower shadow

Low —

Increasing : Bullish Candle Stick

Decreasing : Bearish Candle Stick

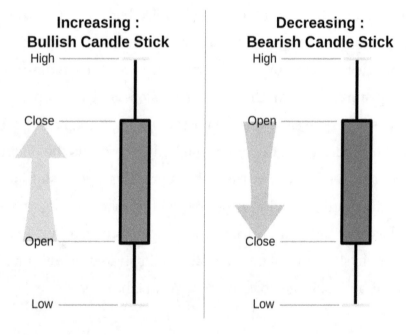

Candlestick Patterns

On some occasions, a single candlestick can indicate a major price shift. There isn't going to be anything to think about when this happens; you will see a very long candlestick body when this occurs. In the case of a price increase, you will see a long green or bullish candlestick that pushes prices to a new level, or you will see a very long price drop with a large red candlestick, pushing prices down to a new level. This can happen on occasion when big news breaks.

But most of the time, a single candlestick does not contain enough information to indicate a trend reversal. There are some exceptions that we will discuss, but in most cases, you are going to look at what two or more candlesticks are doing in terms of forming a pattern, which is a strong indication of a trend reversal. Patterns seen in candlesticks, like the patterns we discussed in the previous two chapters, are strongly indicative but shouldn't be considered in isolation. When you see multiple tools giving you the same signals, then you know there is a real trend reversal in the works, and at that point, you can take action. This action will entail responding to a trend reversal to the upside by buying shares of stock if you are hoping to profit from a price increase. If you are short, then at that time, you also buy them back, to return to the broker, and exit your position. If you are at the top of an uptrend and all the tools you are using point to a trend reversal, if you are long, then it's time to sell your shares to exit the position. If you are looking to go short, you borrow shares from the broker at that point and sell them.

So both long and short investors sell and buy shares at the same time – but when a long investor exits a position, the short investor is entering their position, and when the short investor is exiting their position, the long investor is entering their position.

In the following sections, we will examine some of the candlestick patterns that indicate trend reversals. Candlestick charts are an old tool that can be applied to any financial market. They were originally developed in Japan and used by rice traders. It is interesting to note that anything that is traded is going to follow the same market patterns, from rice to Forex to stocks. Learning candlestick charts is a skill that you can take with you to trade any financial asset.

Engulfing Patterns

The first indicator that we are going to look at with candlestick charts is known as an engulfing pattern. This occurs when a trend has been moving in a certain direction, and then there is a sudden shift in trader sentiment that is demonstrated with a large movement in prices in the opposite direction. The movement in prices is going to be reflected by a large candlestick body, which shows that the closing price moved in a very strong direction opposite to that of the opening price for the trading session.

This is a two-candlestick pattern, so you are looking for a candlestick of one type followed by a candlestick of the opposite type. At the bottom of a downward trend in prices, look for a bearish candlestick followed by a bullish candlestick that has a much larger body. This can be a strong indicator that the trend is going to reverse and be followed by rising prices. If there is an uptrend, you will be looking for a bullish candlestick that is followed by a bearish candlestick with a much larger body. The body of the second candlestick should completely cover, or "engulf" the body of the candlestick that preceded it.

Care should be taken when identifying this or any other candlestick pattern. Always confirm by looking at the overall chart pattern or using technical indicators (in particular moving averages – to be discussed in the next chapter).

The following illustration shows a bullish engulfing pattern, where the bearish candlestick is followed by a large bullish candlestick, that may indicate a coming uptrend in prices.

Bullish Engulfing Pattern

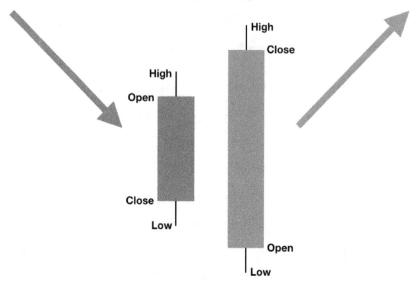

The key characteristics of a bullish engulfing pattern are as follows. While any large bullish candlestick following a smaller bearish candlestick may indicate a coming trend reversal, a true engulfing pattern is going to be one that starts with an opening price that is below the closing price of the previous candlestick. Traders say that the candlestick "gaps lower." Then, the closing price will be much higher than the opening price of the previous trading session and even higher still than the closing price of the previous trading session, such that the length of the bullish candlestick completely covers or "engulfs" the bearish candlestick.

For a bearish engulfing pattern, we look for the two candlesticks reversed, which is a bullish candlestick followed by a bearish candlestick. We also look for the pattern to occur in the midst of an uptrend rather than a downtrend. Again, the body should completely cover the body of the previous, bullish candlestick. In this case, you are going to see the opening of the bearish candlestick shoot higher than the closing of the previous trading session (it will "gap higher"), but then the closing of the bearish candlestick will be lower than the opening of the previous, bullish trading session.

This is illustrated below:

Bearish Engulfing Pattern

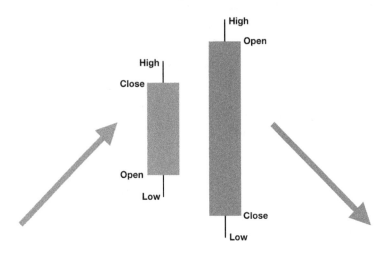

If you see an engulfing pattern, you don't necessarily want to jump right in with the action on your trade. You may want to see what happens in the following trading session. Waiting one more trading session is going to give you enough time to get into a profitable trade or exit a trade if necessary, prices are usually not going to rise or fall very dramatically over the time scales of most candlestick charts used by swing traders in one session (but of course, it can happen). The engulfing pattern is taken to be much stronger or confirmed when the engulfing candlestick is followed by a second candlestick of the same type. That indicates that the trend is actually materializing, and if this is confirmed by other indicators, it can be taken as a time to enter or exit a trade as necessary.

The following illustration shows this pattern that you would seek.

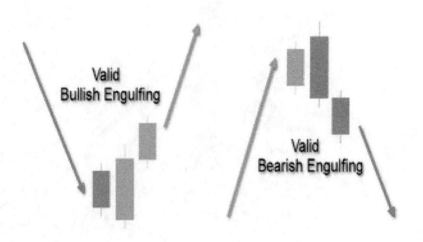

Inverted Hammer

An inverted hammer pattern occurs when you have a small candlestick body, and a long upper wick. An inverted hammer can be either bullish or bearish. If you see an inverted hammer at the bottom of a downtrend, and it's a bullish candlestick, this can be a signal of a coming trend reversal to the upside. So you are going to be looking for a pattern similar to this one:

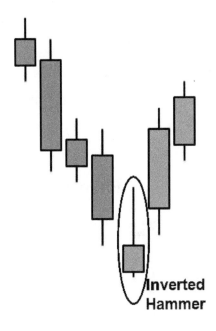

The inverted hammer can be bullish or bearish. This is a one candle pattern, but you should look for the following candles to show an uptrend before taking action or seek confirmation from another indicator or tool.

If the candlestick is bullish, it indicates that the price opened at a relatively low point and was pushed up by buyers bidding up the stock during the trading session, but the momentum couldn't maintain the higher pricing level. Nonetheless, the price closed at a higher level than the opening.

If this type of candle appears at the top of an uptrend, this is known as a shooting star. In this case, you are going to be looking for a bearish candlestick at the top of an uptrend. This indicates that the price was pushed up high, but bears began a selloff, and the priced ended up falling much lower by the end of the trading session, finally closing lower than the opening price. A shooting star is a strong signal of a coming downtrend.

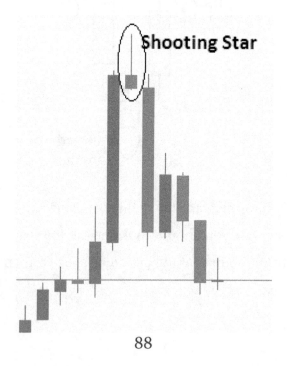

Shooting Star

When you see a shooting star, look for a confirming signal, which would be one or more following candlesticks that are bearish in nature. You can also confirm using other methods.

For a shooting star or inverted hammer, you should see the wick that comes out of the top at least twice as long as the candlestick body, in order for it to have seen enough price pressure to higher prices that dropped down.

Spinning Top

Next, we consider a spinning top, another one candle phenomenon that you should confirm with successive candles. When you have a spinning top, you are going to see a candlestick body with two wicks of equal length coming out of the top and bottom of the candlestick. At the top of an uptrend, a bearish or red spinning top can indicate that a downtrend in prices is coming. In this case, during the trading session, it started at a relatively high price, and prices were pushed even higher, but they were also pushed down and closed at a lower pricing level than both the high price and the opening price of the trading session. The example below shows a bearish spinning top.

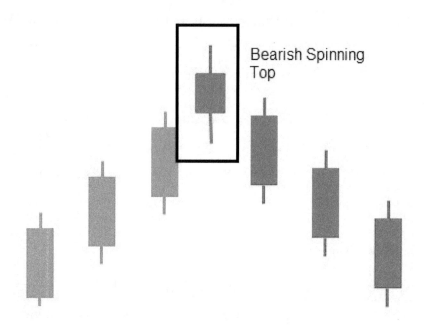

Bearish Spinning Top

You can see in this example that the bearish spinning top is confirmed by three successive bearish candlesticks, each of which has a lower low than the previous candlestick.

A bullish spinning top can occur at the bottom of a downtrend. In this case, although the session opened with a low price, it ended up closing at a higher level. Again, you look for confirming signals such as one or two follow-on bullish candlesticks.

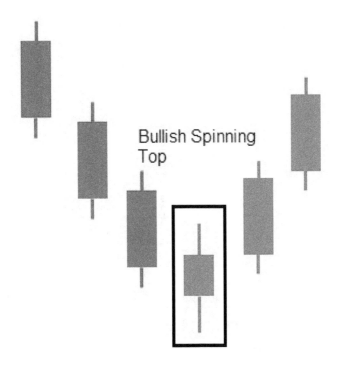

Bullish Spinning Top

Doji

A doji is known as an "indecision candle" in English. The basic meaning of a doji is that traders are indecisive about their mood. There are equal numbers of bears and bulls in the trading session. A doji is indicated by a thin candlestick body, which means that the opening and closing prices of the trading session were exactly the same or nearly so. The candle will have long wicks on either side. For a standard indecision candle, the wicks will be of equal length. Of course, that is the ideal situation. The wicks don't have to be exactly equal to take the candlestick as an indecision candle for all practical purposes. In the image below, we see the shape of an indecision candle.

The best move for a trader to make when they see an indecision candle is to do nothing and adopt a wait and see attitude. You are probably going to have to wait for two or three succeeding trading sessions to play out before you are in a position where making a trading decision is advisable. A doji can be a trend reversal indicator, but you should never act on seeing a doji unless there are following candlesticks confirming the trend reversal and/or you see other signals.

A special type of doji candlestick is known as a "gravestone." This can indicate that a trend reversal might be underway.

With a gravestone, you see that although the opening and closing prices are equal, during the trading session, the price was pushed up very high, relatively speaking. If a gravestone occurs at the top of an uptrend, this can be thought of in terms of a shooting star, although it is not technically so. The same principles appear to be at work, however, indicating that prices were pushed up, but the trend has run out of momentum. In this case, prices may have been pushed up onto late arrivals coming on the scene after a long uptrend, but bears pushed the price back down because the asset is overbought, and so, a sell-off is imminent.

Finally, we have a dragonfly pattern, which is shaped like a hammer, with the long wick below the candlestick body, which in the case of a doji is a thin line indicating similar opening and closing prices for the trading session.

If you see a dragonfly at the top of an uptrend, it can signal a coming downtrend. Likewise, at the bottom of the uptrend, the long wick below the candlestick body can indicate that there may have been some late sellers, but momentum began pushing the share price back up by the end of the trading session, and a trend reversal may follow with upward trending prices.

Marubozu

This type of candlestick consists of a body only. This means that no wicks or shadows will be present at all. If the candlestick is bearish, this means that the low price of the trading session was the closing price, and the high price of the trading session was the opening price. On the other hand, if the candlestick is bullish, this means that the opening price of the trading session was also the lowest price of the trading session, and the high price was the closing price for the trading session.

A marubozu is taken to be a strong signal. Hence, a bullish marubozu is probably an indicator that a rising trend in prices can be expected, while a bearish marubozu probably means that a falling trend in prices can be expected. If it is a bullish or green candle, that means that buyers of the stock were dominant during the trading session. If you can confirm with other signals if you are long on the stock, that is a good time to open your trades to take advantage of future rises in stock price. A bearish marubozu would indicate that those holding stock should sell it and take-profits before the bearish momentum takes hold and really pushes down prices if the current candle didn't already do so.

Bearish Harami

A bearish Harami is a large bullish candle followed by a small bearish candle:

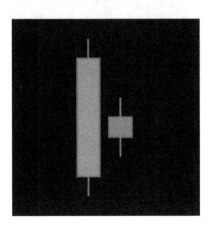

The importance of this pattern is evident in the midst of an uptrend. In that case, the appearance of this seemingly less significant bearish candlestick can be ominous, indicating a potential price reversal. However, this signal isn't a particularly strong one and must be confirmed using other indicators.

Bullish Harami

This is the opposite pattern, a bearish candlestick followed by a small bullish candlestick with equal wicks out the top and bottom. If this occurs at the bottom of a downtrend, it can be a signal of a coming trend reversal. Again, this is something that you are going to want to confirm with other indicators.

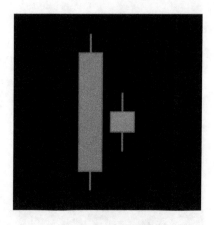

Evening Doji Star

This is a bearish candlestick pattern that you want to watch out for at the top of an uptrend. It is a three-candlestick pattern, that is going to be characterized by a bullish candlestick that is followed by a doji indecision candle that gaps above the bullish candle to a higher price. However, the indecision that is seen indicates that this is the highest price level that is currently attainable, and you can expect a momentum shift and price trend reversal. This suspicion is confirmed if the third candlestick turns out to be a bearish candlestick (image adapted from Proteus on Wikipedia).

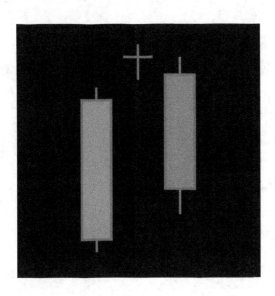

The Morning Star

A morning star pattern is a three-candlestick pattern to look for during a downtrend. Typically, this is going to indicate a reversal into an uptrend. It is characterized by a large bearish candle, followed by a small-bodied bullish candle that has a gap between the closing price of the bearish candle and the closing price of the bullish candle. However, it will have a longer wick to the top, indicating that prices were pushed up by the bullish traders. The next candle should be a bullish candle with a higher closing price that goes up halfway or more above the center of the bearish candlestick on the left, indicating strong momentum in upward price trends.

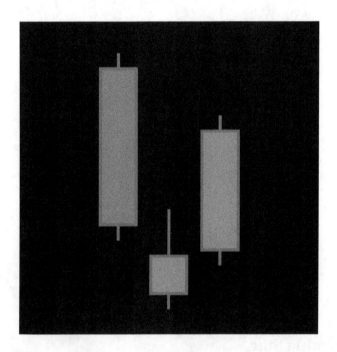

Three Black Crows

The terminology used to describe this pattern is a holdover from when black and white stock charts were used. The key to this pattern is three bearish candlesticks in a row, each with a successive lower closing price than the previous candlestick. This is a very strong indicator that the market is now in a downtrend.

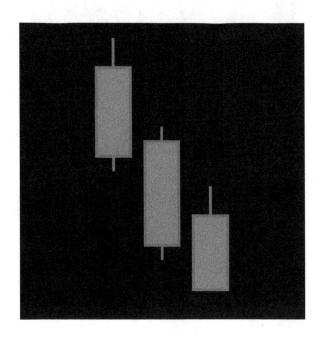

You don't need to pay too much attention to the wicks in this situation. The key is three bearish candlesticks in a row – with lower closing prices at each successive candle.

Three White Soldiers

Like the previous candlestick pattern, the name of this pattern is another holdover from the old days of black and white candlestick charts. In this case, you are looking for three candlesticks in a row that have higher highs in the form of closing prices in succession. This is a strong indication that an uptrend has begun. You can confirm with other signals.

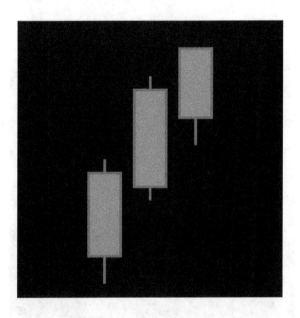

Piercing Line

This is another pattern to look for during a downtrend. A bearish candlestick is followed by a bullish candlestick, which has a lower opening price as compared to the previous close. The line that is "pierced" is the midpoint price of the previous candlestick. So look for the closing price of the bullish candlestick to be past the halfway point of the bearish candlestick. If confirmed by other signals, this usually indicates a price trend reversal has arrived, bringing with it an uptrend in prices.

Rising Window

A rising window is a gap between two bullish candlesticks—that is, the open of the second bullish candlestick is higher than the closing price of the first bullish candlestick. This is an indicator of an uptrend in prices, as the strong momentum is quickly pushing prices up.

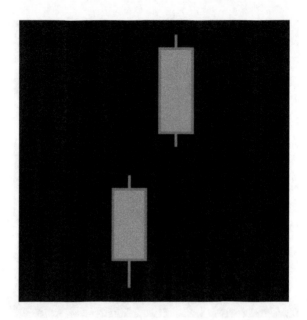

If you see a rising window, this is a strong indicator that if you are looking to profit off rising stock prices, the time to buy is now.

Falling Window

This is the opposite indicator—this time, it's two bearish candlesticks in a row. This time there is a gap down in pricing so that the opening price of the second candlestick is lower than the closing price of the previous candlestick. This tells us that there is strong momentum toward downward pricing pressure. If you have been long on a particular stock at this point, then it is a good time to sell if you see this signal.

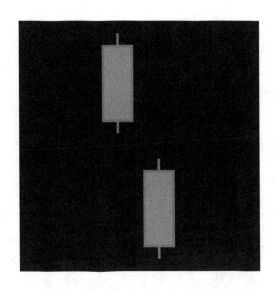

Evening Star

This is a three-candle formation to look for at the top of an uptrend. It usually indicates a trend reversal into falling prices, and so that means that it's time to sell to close your positions if you are long on a stock. The trend includes two bullish candlesticks followed by a bearish candlestick. The bullish middle candlestick shows a lot less pricing movement in that the opening and closing prices are closer to each other as compared to what we see in the other two candlesticks.

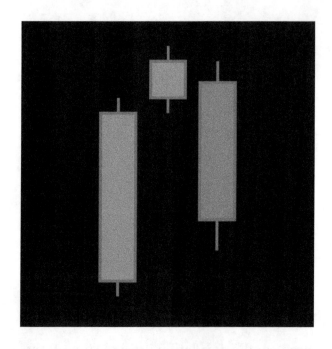

Bullish 3-Formation (Continuation Pattern)

The appearance of the opposite type of candlestick doesn't always represent a downturn, and in a few specific cases, can represent a continuation pattern. By that, we mean that the current trend will resume and continue. One of these patterns that represents this situation is the 3-method pattern. In the bullish case, a bullish candle is followed by three successive bearish candles. They will have lower closing prices in succession. However, the key here is the candlestick bodies will be small in size, relative to the preceding bullish candlestick. The pattern is confirmed when this is followed by a second bullish candlestick that pushes prices back up.

Look for a slightly higher opening price as compared to the last closing price on the three bearish candlesticks, with the closing price of the final bullish candlestick ending higher than all previous opening and closing prices in the sequence. This will occur in the midst of an uptrend and tells us that the uptrend is going to continue. You can consider the three bearish candles to be a false signal.

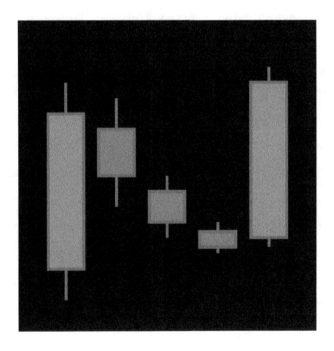

A similar pattern can occur in a downtrend. In that case, you will see a large bearish candlestick followed by three bullish candlesticks in a row, with small bodies. They will each have a higher closing price than the previous bullish candlestick, leading to a momentary mini uptrend. However, this will be followed by a final long-bodied bearish candlestick that resumes the downtrend in prices.

Time Frames Advised For Various Trading Styles

As we mentioned earlier, the time frame that you use in your candlestick charts is going to depend on how long you plan to be in a trade. Of course, you can always use any time frame that you like when analyzing the stock charts. However, there are some basic rules of thumb that are used.

Day traders are going to be making trades over a matter of hours, usually entering a trade in the morning hours or by mid-morning so that they can exit all their trades before the markets close. Since they are basically operating on the edge, day traders are going to be using candlestick charts with trading sessions that are one-minute to five-minutes long. However, a day trader can also get by using a 10 or 15-minute candlestick chart.

For swing traders that are looking at a time horizon of 1-3 days, using 1-hour or 4-hour candlestick charts is appropriate. If you are looking to swing trade over a longer time period of 3-20 days, then you can use an hourly chart, with each candlestick representing a complete hours-worth of trading.

More intermediate time swing traders (who will be staying in their trades longer than 20 days up to a few months in time) can use a daily chart. In this case, the length of a trading session that each candlestick represents would be one trading day.

The longer the time period used to build your candlestick chart, the less sensitive it is going to be against short-term price changes in the data. You can even go so far as to create a weekly chart. A weekly chart is going to combine prices for an entire week into a single candlestick, so you can look at a candlestick showing prices for an entire Monday through Friday period. The opening price will be the opening price on Monday morning, and the closing price for the candlestick will give you the closing price on Friday afternoon. The wicks of the candlestick are going to show you the high and low prices for the entire week.

A weekly chart can be very useful for swing traders. It reduces the amount of noise that is in the data. As you probably know quite well, stock market data is quite noisy, meaning there are lots of ups and downs in the data that are meaningless as far as the long-term trend of the stock price is concerned. If you are going to stay in a particular stock longer than 10 days, having a look at weekly charts makes sense. This is because it will remove the noise and allow you to focus on the actual trend in the stock price. As a swing trader, having a fix on the trend, especially if you are going to stay in the stock for several weeks, is going to be very important. Generally speaking, weekly charts are only useful to long-term investors, but they can help you get in on a long-term trend and make estimates on when to exit the trade.

When doing long-term trends, be sure to be aware of important dates that can have a large influence on the stock price. There are many things to keep track of in the general economy, such as unemployment rates, inflation, interest rates, and GDP growth. However, the most important time for a specific stock, barring unsettling international or political events that impact the entire stock market, are earnings calls. An earnings call can cause a complete reset of the pricing level, and so, it's usually best to get out of your positions in the days leading up to an earnings call, and then wait until after the earnings call—probably the week after—for the dust to settle. Once the dust has settled, then you can get into new trades.

Of course, there is a chance that the current trend will continue past the earnings call if the results are consistent with the present trend. However, that can be a pretty risky proposition to bet your finances on. There can be times when you will be able to get extremely lucky, and the results announced in the earnings call work in your favor. For example, if there is an upward trend in pricing, and the announced results exceed the expectations of analysts, then the upward trend will significantly strengthen, and you will find that your bet pays off. However, these times are extremely finicky. A company can announce profitable results, but if it doesn't beat the predictions of analysts, then share prices might actually drop. As absurd as this is, that is the way the markets work. Hence, my own personal opinion is to avoid being in a trade when there is an earnings call. You just take a few days off.

Trading on multiple time frames can actually help you get the biggest payoff. As a swing trader, this means you can trade over 1-3 days, 3-20 days, and up to several weeks simultaneously. As far as candlestick charts go, this means that you will be utilizing many different lengths for your trading sessions. You can do multiple trades on different time frames for the same or for multiple stocks. Personally, I don't like to put all my eggs in one basket and so stick to using many different stocks. Some are going to turn out to be the losers, but that is just the nature of the game.

Chapter 5: Mission-Critical Technical Indicators

In this chapter, we are going to investigate technical indicators. These are add-ons to stock market charts that provide important information that can be used to estimate when there are going to be trend reversals and the strength of trends. These are normally used in conjunction with candlestick charts. The candlestick chart can be seen as the main workhorse of the swing trader. And the technical indicators are used to confirm the signals seen in the candlestick charts, helping the prepared trader move effectively on a trade.

Moving Averages

The moving average is one of the most important if not the most important technical indicator used by swing traders. A moving average is a simple concept. At each point on a stock market chart, a point defined as a trading session that you are using, it calculates the average of the past x-trading periods and plots the result. What you get is a smoothed-out curve that removes the noise from the pricing data. Normally, the closing price is used to compute the average.

A swing trader will incorporate two moving averages on their stock chart. The behavior of the moving averages relative to one another will provide signals that indicate when there is going to be a trend reversal. This method is quite effective, and it requires using two moving averages. One is a short period moving average, and one is a long period moving average. There are different ways that this can be done, but one popular method is to use a 9-period moving average together with a 20-period moving average on your stock chart at the same time.

In the sample chart below, the smooth blue line is a moving average. You can see how it produces a smooth curve that reveals the trend in the pricing data, getting rid of all the jagged short term and basically meaningless price swings.

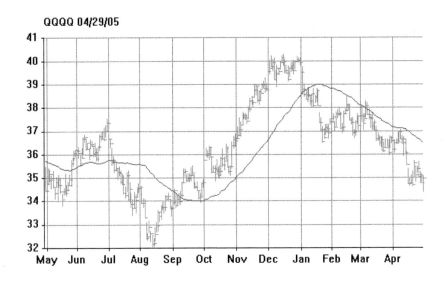

There are many different moving averages available that use different algorithms. A simple moving average simply computes the arithmetic mean of the number of points specified. Many traders are happy with simple moving averages, but some are not because they treat all prices the same. That is, if you had a 30 day moving average, the price of the stock 30 days ago is treated the same as yesterday's closing price, but we know that the closing price yesterday has a lot more relevance to tomorrow's price, and so a simple moving average isn't really the best way to do the calculation.

The way to get around this is to weight the prices so that the more recent prices have more weight than prices in the more distant past. One tool you can use for this purpose is the exponential moving average. Exponential moving averages tend to produce more accurate curves. An even more accurate version is called the Hull moving average. Most traders use exponential moving averages.

Crossovers Of Moving Averages

The important thing to look for with moving averages, no matter what type you use, are crossovers. The attention is focused on the shorter-term moving average and its behavior with respect to the long-term moving average. If you are using one-hour trading sessions, then you can use a 9-period moving average that will give you the average of the closing prices for the last 9 hours. Then, you can also add a 20-period moving average to the chart that has the average of the closing prices over the last 20 hours of trading.

Golden Cross

If the short-period moving average crosses above the long-period moving average, this is known as a golden cross. It's called golden because this crossover is a signal that an upward trend in prices is forming. So what is typically done is a trader is using a candlestick chart with the moving averages, and you will look for the formation of a known candlestick pattern that indicates a trend reversal, and you will see if the golden cross also occurs for confirmation. Often they will occur at the same time, but with the two in agreement, you can have confidence that you are making the right trading move.

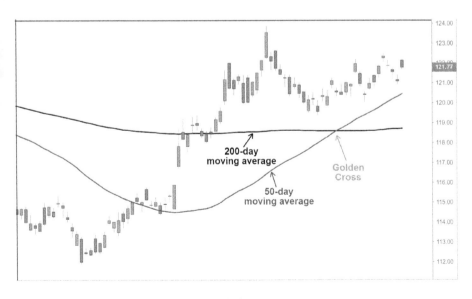

The choice of moving averages will depend on your time frame, or more particularly, on the time frame used for the candlesticks versus the time frame you are looking to use for the trade. The most popular choices are 9-period and 20-period, and 50-period and 200-period.

Death Cross

The death cross occurs when the short-period moving average dips below the long-period moving average. The meaning of this is that a downturn in prices can be expected. If the stock has been in an upward trend, if you see a death cross, a trend reversal is very likely. You can use it to confirm patterns seen in the candlestick chart.

Daily Chart of AAPL from January 2012 to December 2013
With 50-Day and 200-Day Moving Averages

BarHLC, AAPL.O, Trade Price
1/5/2017, 116.864200, 115.810000, 116.200000, +0.180000, (+0.16%)
SMA, AAPL.O, Trade Price(Last), 50
1/5/2017, 112.764800
SMA, AAPL.O, Trade Price(Last), 200
1/5/2017, 106.364200

Chart courtesy of Thomson Reuters Eikon

Bollinger Bands

Another popular tool used by swing traders is the Bollinger Bands tool. This tool is a very powerful tool that gives you three pieces of information on one chart. There are three curves or bands that are included on the chart when you use Bollinger bands. The middle curve is a simple moving average (but you can set options on this with most stock market charts). Above and below the moving average, you will see two more curves. These curves mark the points two standard deviations above and below the moving average. If the price is not really going to change dramatically, it can be expected to stay within two standard deviations of the mean. But when you see the candlesticks touching or even moving outside one of the standard deviation curves, this is an indication that a trend reversal is coming. So if the market has been in a downward trend, and you see the candlesticks going outside the lower standard deviation curve, this can be an indication that a trend reversal is in the works. You can check the patterns in the candlesticks in order to confirm this hypothesis or reject it. Likewise, if the candlesticks are moving outside the top standard deviation, it is expected that the prices are going to revert back to the mean, and so there will be a downward trend.

Basically, Bollinger bands are a mean reversion indicator. The purpose of this is to get boundaries that determine how far a price will move in one direction or another before there is a retracement.

Of course, there are going to be many occasions when the price is going to break out of the current bounds that are associated with the stock. This means that if you are using Bollinger bands, keeping a close eye on the patterns in the candlestick charts is crucial. For example, the stock may be in a breakout to a higher pricing level, and so when it's touching the upper band, it might actually move to a higher price rather than signal a trend reversal. However, the chart below illustrates quite nicely how the trend reversals are usually indicated when the prices touch or go outside the standard deviation curves.

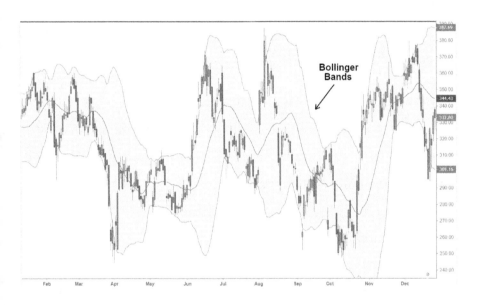

Technical Indicators — Best Practices

We are going to be continuing our discussion of technical indicators. But the fact is you have already learned 90% of what you need to know in order to be successful in doing swing trading. Let's begin with candlestick charts. They contain a wealth of information that is extremely useful in doing your analysis. Using that in conjunction with moving averages is often all you need.

Also, don't forget that many traders, some of whom are extremely successful, just focus on chart patterns. If you learn the chart patterns that typically indicate trend reversals and combine this with knowledge gleaned from the candlestick charts, this can be quite a lot of information that can help you be a successful trader.

In the end, you will have to pick and choose the tools that you personally feel are going to help you be the most successful trader you can be. Some traders will feel like using all the tools that are available actually gets in the way. Indeed, in many cases, you are going to find that some of the tools actually provide redundant information, and you can make things cloudy by piling on too many indicators and graphs. Another thing to consider is that when you are paying attention to a large number of indicators, you might find that you are in a situation where you're actually overwhelmed by information, and you become indecisive.

So study and read up on all the tools that are available and then make your decisions based on personal taste. In my opinion, using candlestick charts with moving averages is all the information that is needed to get the right entry and exit points for trades. Others swear by Bollinger bands, and others are constantly looking for Gartley patterns. Many people find Gartley patterns too constraining and too much work. In the end, the key to success is using some tools that provide you with reliable information—rather than making trades that are based on nothing more than gut instinct.

Chapter 6: 6 Essential Axioms Of Wall Street And How To Quantify The Market Sentiment

In this chapter, we are going to continue our investigation into more technical indicators and tools that can be used for market analysis. We will begin our discussion with polarity.

Polarity

Polarity is a way to measure market sentiment, and this can be used to help you determine the right time to enter or exit a trade. The idea behind polarity is that there exists an imbalance between buyers and sellers at any given time in the market. To take an example, consider that recently Google saw a major drop in profit because of increasing expenses. This drop-in profit, as you might guess, caused a major downward trend in prices. Why? From the point of view of polarity, it's because in a situation like that, there are going to be far more sellers than buyers of Google. With more sellers, simple supply and demand dictate that the prices are going to drop.

Polarity seeks to measure market sentiment and determine how that impacts the formation of market trends. In polarity, price is the most important indicator of all. Price is a reflection of the underlying supply and demand, and hence of trends.

Back To Support And Resistance: Polarity Psychology

Support and resistance create psychological barriers in the market, often reinforcing themselves in doing so. Let's explain how this works. Remember that support is a bottom price that a stock won't go below over a certain time period. It is the lowest level price that the market has assigned as far as the value of that stock, and unless there is some change in circumstances that would make the pricing point unjustifiably high for the intrinsic value of the stock, such as a bad earnings report, the odds of the stock going below the support price level are low.

People internalize this number. They also internalize the resistance pricing level. Remember that resistance is the high price that unless circumstances in the market change, the stock never seems to cross. So for a period of time, the stock is going to be ranging between the support and resistance prices.

Now, if you get interested in a stock, you might start watching it. Suppose that you are watching Apple, and it's trading at $210 a share. Then, you see Apple rise in price for a couple of weeks, reaching $230 a share. At this point, you are filled with regret, having missed the proverbial buy-low and sell-high opportunity. But then the stock, which is really in ranging behavior, begins to decline again. Pretty soon, you see it's dropped to $210 a share. It bounces around this price for a few days.

At this point, you think that now is a great chance to get in on Apple. You lucked out, and the stock price dropped again, and life doesn't have many second chances.

So you buy 100 shares of Apple. You start feeling good, and many other people who were watching the stock were making the same observations. So they buy in too. This is crowd behavior 101.

Now with increasing demand, the price is going back up. Over a few weeks, it gets back to $230 a share. Many traders are going to start feeling a psychological pull at this point because they have seen the stock reversed course and drop down to the lower price again, once it reaches the $230 price level. Even professional traders are going to be getting ready to sell their shares at this point because they study market behavior and believe the stock is ranging.

So in a fit of self-fulfilling prophecy, many traders, maybe even including you, start selling their shares. They make a nice profit if they had gotten in at $210 a share, and with all the selling, the price starts dropping. A change in market sentiment because of previous observations actually creates a trend that keeps the stock ranging.

The Principle Of Polarity

Now consider the situation where one of the pricing levels is breached. When there is a breakout in pricing, this blows apart the psychology of the previous scenario. The principle of polarity tells us that the psychology of traders is going to change when the level of resistance or support is breached. If there is a breakout to the upside, then the previous level of resistance becomes the new level of support. This is the principle of polarity.

The principle of polarity also works to the downside. Sometimes, bad news related to a company is going to cause the price of its stock to hit a major decline. When this happens, oftentimes, the previous level of support becomes the new pricing level of resistance.

When the resistance level becomes the new support level, this happens because demand has exceeded supply. Vice versa, when the previous level of support becomes the new level of resistance, that happens because supply is outstripping demand.

Polarity: Volume By Price

Remember, we discussed that traders are going to be interested in getting out of their positions when the price reaches the resistance pricing level. If circumstances are right, when they are unloading their positions, new buyers are going to come in to take up that supply. If external circumstances warrant it, the volume of buyers coming in is going to exceed the supply being dumped at the resistance pricing level. This will lead to a breakout to the upside.

This can also happen during a breakout to the downside. As traders are dumping their holdings, the volume can increase as the price is moving to the support level. Now suppose that there is bad news about the stock or the economy. Now other traders that would hold their positions begin dumping their stock as well. The volume begins increasing, leading to a breakout to the downside as supply exceeds demand by a large margin.

Polarity Example

Consider the stock for Netflix, which has had two bad inflection points in 2019. They were both the result of bad earnings calls, where investors were sorely disappointed by declining numbers of subscribers. Prior to the first earnings call, we see that the stock was stable, with clear levels of support and resistance. The earnings call is a classic example of polarity volume by price in action. After the bad earnings call, the volume of traders unloading their shares was massive, causing a significant price drop to a new level of support. In fact, it ended up well below the previous level. You can see from the chart that this continued to the second earnings call, where there was a second breakout to the downside.

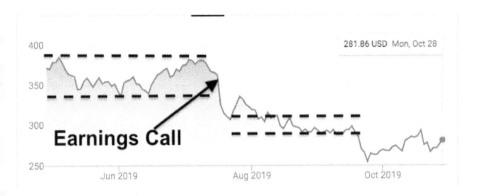

Although not quite matching up, you see that the previous level of support is not far off from the level of resistance following the earnings call.

SNAP actually illustrates the opposite behavior. In July, they had a better earnings call than Netflix, which resulted in a break to the upside as volume increased, and the previous level of resistance became the new level of support, in a near-classic example of polarity.

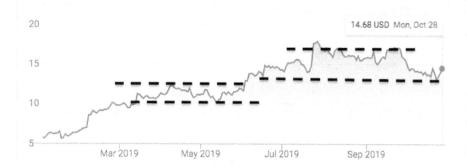

Dow Theory History

The Dow Theory is a branch of technical analysis developed by Charles Dow in the late 19th century. It has six basic tenets. The first important part of the Dow Theory is that the market has three main movements. This is important for swing traders. The main movement is a major trend that can last from about a year to several years. You can see long-term trends in any stock that you pick that last over long time periods.

Market Trends

The second movement is the medium swing. The medium swing is a short-term swing in prices that lasts from ten days up to three months. As a swing trader, this can be important to focus on. It will retrace 33% to 66% of the price changes since the start of the main movement that is currently in force.

Finally, there are short swings, also of interest to swing traders and day traders. Short swings are price swings that last from hours to a month. While the main movement could be bullish, there can be bearish short swings and vice versa.

The second tenet of the theory is that any market trend goes through three phases. The first phase is called the accumulation phase. This is when professional investors are buying up a stock because they are "in the know" before the market at large thinks that the stock is a good buy. Soon enough, people notice what's happening, and the second phase begins, which is the public participation phase. This is when the general public follows along behind the in the know investors and start buying into the stock, pushing up prices further. In fact, they can push prices up much higher since the demand for the stock is increased to high levels, eventually leading to speculation. Then, the market enters a distribution phase. In this case, smart investors start dumping their shares, recognizing that prices are peaking. This, in turn, leads to downward pressure on pricing.

The third tenet of Dow Theory is that the stock market follows the efficient market hypothesis. That means that the market will incorporate news into pricing as soon as the news is available. You certainly see this today – as soon as important news hits the markets respond.

The fourth tenet of Dow Theory is that indexes in the markets will confirm each other. That is related sectors will move together in the markets. The key example used here by Dow was the relationship between big manufacturing companies and the transportation sector, which must ship raw materials and supplies to the manufacturing companies, and in turn, ship finished goods to the market. They must move in tandem.

Fifth, pricing trends, if real and significant, are going to be confirmed by volume. If the volume isn't there, the trend may not be real. For example, price movements that are not accompanied by high volume might occur because one institutional trader is making a move. It won't be sustainable.

Averages Dictate Everything

Finally, Dow focused on avoiding market noise, and the tenet states that trends continue until technical indicators and signals demonstrate that they are reversing. You see this today in the application of moving averages.

DJTA

The Dow Jones Transportation Average is an index of transportation, including railroad, shipping, and air freight carriers. This index is published by leading financial news organizations because it follows the fourth tenet of Dow theory.

Although the US has become a more service-oriented economy, the DJTA is still very significant since consumer goods still need to be shipped. They are shipped into the country and also within the country to warehouses and then to market, and so, this is still an important indicator.

DJIA

The Dow Jones Industrial Average is an index that tracks the 30 largest publicly traded companies on US stock exchanges. It was originally compiled as a part of Dow theory, to compliment the DJTA by compiling an index of manufacturing companies when the United States was primarily a manufacturing economy, and the fourth tenet of Dow theory indicated that industrial companies and transportation companies must be moving in tandem given the health of the economy. In today's world, the DJIA has evolved, because many of the largest companies in the United States are no longer primarily manufacturing companies. For example, American Express, a financial company, is on the DJIA. So is Merck, which is a pharmaceutical company. The DJIA is far more diverse than it was in Dow's time, and the S & P 500 has become a more reliable indicator for the overall health of the market than the DJIA, but the DJIA still remains closely tracked by most investors.

Closing Prices

The closing price is one of the most important prices for investors. It is taken as the reference point for stock behavior. If you pull up a stock market chart, the default setting, no matter how much time you select for your trading session, is going to default to displaying closing prices. When determining the performance of a stock over any time period, the closing prices are used. This is true whether you are using a week, a month, or a year to examine the performance of a stock. Opening prices are not taken to be as significant because, during the first 30 minutes of the trading day, there can be a lot of short-term stock price movement, some of it occurring in the instance of market opening, that is not going to last. By closing time, the prices have settled down and more accurately reflect the true value of the stock on that day.

Bull Markets

A bull market is a market of rising prices, which is tied together with a good economy. The tie is not exact; you can have a stagnant market and even a bear market while there is decent GDP growth. But in most cases, rising stock prices are going to correlate to a good economy. During a bull market, most, but not all, stocks will be rising steadily in price. This rising price trend is going to be the main trend that the stocks are following.

There will, of course, be ups and downs in the middle of the good overall trend, but during a bull market, the majority of stocks and the major indices are going to be displaying long term upward trends in prices. The DJIA and S & P 500, in particular, are going to have a particular trend that is increasing during a bull market.

Bear Markets

Bear markets often, but not always, correspond to a recession in the economy. During a bear market, most stocks are going to be in a downward trend in price. The major stock indices like the DJIA and S & P 500 will be declining, as investors are shedding their stock holdings to move into safer investments like cash and bonds. Many long-term investors see bear markets as buying opportunities because bear markets are temporary, and you can get a stock at a discount that is going to rise to higher pricing levels later.

Chapter 7: Decoding Supplemental Indicators

There are many other indicators that can be used to do technical analysis. Again, it's important to avoid overdoing it. Many of the indicators are redundant. However, you may want to use indicators that help you determine the volume and overbought or oversold conditions. In this chapter, we will review some of these supplemental indicators that you can use to get more insight into trading and finding the right times to buy and sell your holdings.

Secondary Indicators

There are a few secondary indicators that can give you an overview of trends happening in the overall market, including price trends, and volume.

The first secondary indicator that traders can use is the Advance/Decline line. This is a general indicator that will tell you what the majority of stocks in the market are doing—in other words, how many stocks are following the major stock indexes, as well as how many are going against the major stock indexes. The plot itself uses the numbers of advancing shares against the number of declining shares.

The Bulls vs. Bears ratio is a ratio of the number of bulls to the number of bears among a select polled group of professional traders. This indicator will give you an idea of the sentiment of professional traders on the market. As the indicator increases, this tells you that among professional traders, the mood is bullish, and so they are expecting increasing stock prices. If the indicator is dropping, that tells you that the mood among professional traders is bearish, and they are expecting declining stock prices.

Another secondary indicator is the 10-day moving average up & down volume. This indicator gives you an idea of the volume of shares trading that are moving up in price and the volume of the shares trading that are decreasing in price. These are shown on a graph with two different curves, one line for the stocks moving up, and one line for the stocks moving down. This secondary indicator will help you get a handle on the overall trading mood on the market.

Next, we consider the 10-day moving average of new highs and lows. These plots will show you the number of stocks that are reaching new highs and another plot showing the moving average of stocks reaching new lows. As with other moving averages, look for crossovers that can indicate changing trends in the overall markets.

The short-interest ratio is a secondary indicator for the New York Stock Exchange (NYSE). This gives the ratio of short interest to average daily volume. If the ratio is increasing, this means that the overall sentiment on the NYSE is negative. If the ratio is decreasing, this means that the overall sentiment on the NYSE is positive.

Moving Average Convergence-Divergence (MACD) Indicator

The moving average convergence-divergence indicator is an "oscillator" that performs a function similar to that of using two moving averages to look for crossovers. This indicator consists of two lines and a histogram. The first line is called the signal line. There is also the MACD line, which is the primary line to pay attention to if you are using this indicator. Checking the value of the MACD, you want to determine if it is below or above zero. When the MACD is above zero, this indicates bullish conditions. The MACD crossing above zero can be taken as a buy signal. When the MACD is below zero, this is taken as a bearish signal. If you see the MACD decline below zero, then this is an indication that you should sell your holdings.

You can also compare the MACD line to the signal line. The technique here is similar to that used with moving averages. When the MACD crosses above the signal line, this is a bullish signal. Therefore, when this happens, you want to enter your positions and buy stocks if you are looking to enter a long position.

When the MACD crosses below the signal line, this is a bearish indicator. So this is equivalent to a death cross that you would see using two moving averages. Therefore, if you are long on a stock, you want to sell your position if the MACD crosses below the signal line.

The MACD is actually calculated using two exponential moving averages, so this is really a fancy tool that plays the same role as using moving averages. Generally speaking, you subtract the 26-period moving average from a 12-period moving average. The signal line is actually constructed by creating a 9-period moving average of the MACD line. Different values can be used for the periods if desired, but this is the typical setup that is used.

The Relative Strength Index (RSI)

One of the most popular supplemental indicators is the Relative Strength Index, which goes by the abbreviation RSI. The purpose of the relative strength index is to help you determine whether or not there are overbought or oversold conditions for any given stock. Overbought conditions happen when too many buyers have bid up the stock price past values that are justified given the actual value of the stock. When there are overbought conditions since the price of the shares has been pushed up higher than the actual value of the company would indicate is justified, and so traders are going to start selling their positions, and this will lead to a cascade of selling, leading to a trend reversal.

Oversold conditions occur when selling off of the shares occurs to a point where the price of the stock is pushed to levels that are lower than they should be given the actual worth of the stock. At this point, traders who recognize the value of obtaining the stock at discount prices, and so they start buying up shares. As this happens, a trend reversal starts forming, and this attracts more investors.

The value of the relative strength index ranges from 0 to 100. When the indicator ranges between 0 and 30, this indicates oversold conditions. Therefore, when the RSI is below 30, and you see signs of a trend reversal with your other indicators, if you are looking to go long on a stock, this is a time to buy shares to enter your position. Those who are shorting their stock can buy back shares to return the broker at this point.

If the RSI goes above 70, this indicates overbought conditions. If the other indicators that you are using show a trend reversal, then those who are long should exit their positions by selling the stock. If you are looking to short, then it is a good time to borrow shares to sell on the market.

It is important not to use the RSI in isolation, or to make a trading move based on the value of the RSI. In many cases, if the RSI goes into overbought conditions, for example, the stock price can keep rising for a long period afterward. So in many cases, you can use the RSI as a "get ready" signal. Once you see the RSI go above 70, then start paying close attention to chart patterns, the signals seen in candlestick charts, and the moving averages to look for a crossover that would tell you to sell your position.

Likewise, if the RSI drops below 30, that doesn't mean that you should automatically buy shares. Prices of the stock may continue to decline sometime after the RSI has indicated oversold conditions. So, as you would in the case of an uptrend, look for a golden cross in your moving averages. You can also look for the right time to buy into a position by keeping a close eye on the candlestick charts.

14-Day RSI

Typically, the RSI is used with a 14-day time frame. If you are using the 14-day RSI, and the value goes below 30, this is a bullish signal that should be confirmed using other indicators.

On the other hand, if the 14-Day RSI goes above 70, then this is a bearish signal that should be confirmed with other indicators. The RSI is considered to be a momentum indicator. To learn what momentum refers to, read the next section.

Momentum Divergence

A key concept in technical analysis of stock markets is price momentum. The amount of price momentum depends on the length of time that there is when there is a short-term price swing. Understanding these amounts to a bit of common sense. If the price swing happens over a short time period, then there is a high level of price momentum. If the price swing happens over a longer time period, then there is a lower level of price momentum.

The slope of a pricing curve is going to be large in magnitude, or steep on the graph. In contrast, if the amount of momentum is low, then the slope will be smaller in magnitude, which means that the graph will be shallow.

There are three main momentum indicators used by professional traders. We have already encountered the first of these, the relative strength index, or RSI. Other momentum indicators include stochastics and rate of change.

Divergence is a phenomenon when momentum is divergent from the indicators.

Momentum is important when interpreting a trend. If the momentum is weak, this indicates that the trend is going to be less stable. Suppose that the trend is an uptrend in price. If the momentum is weak, the upward trend in prices may halt, leading to a phenomenon of consolidation where prices are not changing significantly. Alternatively, if momentum is weak, the trend is also weak, and it can reverse.

The longer a swing in prices, the more momentum the trend has. Using momentum indicators will help you get a smoothed out curve of trending that will help you determine this more accurately. You can also get this type of information using a short-period moving average. The Hull moving average is particularly good for this purpose.

Divergence occurs when you see the trend in the indicator moving in a different way as the trend in the price of the stock. For example, suppose that the price is on an uptrend, but the RSI is down trending. This is an example of divergence. Alternatively, we could see prices declining, but an upward trend in the RSI, indicating a move toward overbought conditions even though the price is declining.

Momentum indicators and seeking signs of divergence is not valid when a stock is in ranging conditions. This is because the trends in ranging conditions are not strong enough. The best time to use momentum indicators is during breakout conditions and trend reversal conditions.

Bullish Conditions

At this point, we can discuss what a momentum divergence means. The typical interpretation of a momentum divergence is that there will be a price retracement. Therefore, if prices have been rising, and you see a divergence in the momentum indicator, this can be an indication that you should sell your position.

Often, a divergence will indicate a situation where there is going to be a pullback in prices that is temporary, and it will be followed by a resumption of the trend. At other times, it can indicate that ranging behavior is soon to follow. In some cases, momentum divergence can actually be followed by a trend reversal.

Bearish Conditions

A momentum divergence from price applies in bearish conditions as well. Again, this can indicate a price retracement. It can indicate a good time to buy when entering a long position.

The divergence can indicate that a price increase is coming. The bottom line is that you are going to be wanting to look at other indicators and signals.

Parabolic SAR

The parabolic SAR is another useful indicator that you may wish to include in your technical analysis. This is a curve that you can overlay on top of your stock chart. The curve will either be above or below the prices of the stock. If the stock is in an uptrend, and the parabolic SAR is below the price curve, this indicates that you have reached a point of a trend reversal, and a downward trend in prices is going to follow. If you are in a downward trend in prices, and the parabolic SAR moves above the price curve, this is an indication that a trend reversal is developing that will lead to a coming uptrend. The parabolic SAR can be a very useful tool, and confidence in what it is telling you can be increased by using it in conjunction with other indicators.

Volume By Price

Trading volume, besides price action, can be very important to help you determine whether or not a trend is real or not. Volume by price is a histogram that you can include on your stock chart to give you the amount of volume there is at each price point. This will allow you to determine how many traders are getting in on the action at each pricing level. When volume is low, that can indicate that you should wait and see what happens before making major moves on your trades.

Average Directional Index

Of all the supplemental tools, this is one that deserves a look. The main purpose of this tool is to help you determine whether or not a stock is trending or if the stock is entering a period of range. Of course, looking back in time, it's easy to see when a stock is ranging, but when you are in the midst of trading, it's not always so easy to determine.

The ADX is actually used with two other indicators. These are the minus directional indicator, which is sometimes denoted by -DI, and the plus directional indicator that is denoted by +DI. The minus directional indicator gives you the difference between respective lows, and the positive directional indicator gives you the difference between respective highs. In other words, at each point, -DI gives you the current low minus the previous low, and +DI gives you the current high minus the previous high. The ADX takes the difference between the plus directional indicator and the minus directional indicator and then calculates the smoothed average.

The ADX is going to give you the strength of the trend. To know the direction of the trend, you will rely on the +DI and -DI curves.

Types Of Indicators And Guide On What To Use

Indicators can be leading or lagging. The first thing to consider when choosing which technical indicators to use is you should select some leading indicators and some lagging indicators.

An example of a leading indicator is the Relative Strength Index or RSI. Remember that we mentioned that sometimes the RSI is going to indicate overbought or oversold conditions, but the trend is going to continue on for some time. This is because the RSI is a leading indicator. Leading indicators are going to indicate a trend reversal before it actually happens. So a leading indicator is going to tell you where the price will go in the future. A lagging indicator will indicate a change after it's already started. Other leading indicators include momentum and some volume indicators.

Lagging indicators include trend indicators, moving averages, and mean reversion. The chief lagging indicators you are going to use are moving averages. You might also use Bollinger bands.

When choosing which indicators to use, you should keep things to a minimum. But if you want to use a maximal set of indicators, you should make sure that you avoid duplication. There is no point in using multiple indicators that provide the same information. Therefore, using MACD and moving averages is really providing duplicate trend information. You should use moving averages OR the MACD.

Technical indicators are grouped into four different types, besides being classified as leading or lagging. The four types are trend, momentum, volume, and volatility. So the ideal situation is to have one indicator of each of the types.

Professional advisors also recommend that you try and get a mix of leading and lagging indicators. That is why the RSI is a good indicator to include with your analysis, as it is going to give you a good and reliable leading indication of coming changes in price trends. So to start with, either go with two moving average that you can put on your chart to look for golden and death crosses. Although this trend indicator is a lagging indicator, the trend is not going to go very far before you see the crossing, and you can be in a relatively confident situation if you are able to confirm the crossings you see with patterns in the candlestick charts.

Alternatively, if you are going to use the MACD, there is not really any point in using moving averages.

Then, the RSI is probably one of the most important tools to include. This will give you a combination of leading and lagging indicators that are going to help you get a handle on trend reversals.

These tools can be complemented with volume and volatility indicators.

Once you settle on a set of indicators, you should run them through a testing period. Don't be afraid to change out indicators that aren't working out for you. We have described the major indicators that are most frequently used by professional traders, but due to space limitations, we have left out several others. This indicates that you have a homework assignment, which is to give yourself a thorough education in all of the technical indicators so that you understand them all and can find the best mix of indicators that work for you.

And as we have said, using technical indicators is not going to be for everyone. Not all traders have the same style, and many traders don't use indicators at all, or they use a bare-bones set of technical indicators. We have said this before, but there can be an "art or science" approach to trading. When you are relying more on chart patterns, then you are taking an approach that views trading as an art. These types of traders may use clean charts. You can have a clean chart as a line chart, bar chart, or candlestick chart. When you take this approach, you can focus on the patterns you see in the stock charts in order to make your trading decisions. This can be done looking for trend reversal patterns, such as the head and shoulders or double top, and by looking for ABCD patterns. This can be done with or without candlesticks.

Candlesticks alone can provide a wealth of information. But whenever you are trading in real-time, there are always going to be false signals. And if you are in a situation where you need to get in and out of trades quickly, relying on candlestick charts can be less valuable. That doesn't mean you wouldn't want to use candlestick charts; you will probably want to use them under all circumstances. But you can really get a lot more out of candlestick charts by using moving averages with them.

Whether novice traders should use a lot of technical indicators or not is kind of a double-edged sword. Those with less experience trading stocks can benefit from having more information at their fingertips. On the other hand, a novice trader can get overwhelmed by having a lot of information available, and they can also suffer from a lack of understanding.

Given those possibilities, if you are a new swing trader and you haven't done technical analysis before, it is my recommendation that you start off simple and learn each tool thoroughly before moving on to adding more tools to your analysis. You should even spend some time doing stock analysis without actually entering into trades. During that phase, consider only studying line charts of stocks so that you can start to train yourself to recognize the various patterns that we have talked about in the book. This can be done both in real-time and by simply looking back at older stock charts.

Once you have familiarized yourself with the patterns in real-time, then you can move on from line charts to using candlesticks, and again, practice before entering real trades. Study candlestick charts and spend some time watching them build up in real-time and look for the patterns you need to look for in order to determine when there are going to be trend reversals.

Chapter 8: Fibonacci Retracement Secrets

Fibonacci retracement is an advanced technique that is used by some technical traders. It is also the math that is behind the Gartley and ABCD charts that we visited earlier in the book. Most traders don't need to understand the details of the mathematics behind the ratios used in ABCD charts. But for those that are interested, understanding the Fibonacci retracement can equip you with another tool that will help you be better placed to make more winning trades.

The purpose of using Fibonacci retracement in association with stock charts is to determine levels of price support and resistance. This can help you determine your entry and exit points for the trade. Fibonacci retracement, like any other technical indicator, should not be used in isolation. Use it in conjunction with other tools of analysis, such as moving averages and your candlestick chart patterns.

The Fibonacci Problem And Fibonacci Sequences

Fibonacci came up with a sequence of numbers that has surprisingly been found to have applications in multiple areas, from nature to the stock market and beyond. This is called a Fibonacci sequence. A Fibonacci sequence starts at 0 or 1, and then each number in the sequence is formed from the sum of the previous two numbers. It approximates a logarithmic spiral series, and in nature, can be used to describe shapes such as the shell of a snail.

The number 1.618 is known as Phi, and it is known as the basis of the "golden ratio." Each number in a Fibonacci sequence is approximately 1.618 times as large as the preceding number.

There are actually many Fibonacci ratios. These are the key Fibonacci ratios. For the application of stocks or other financial markets, they are expressed as percentages. The important Fibonacci ratios for stock charts are 23.6%, 38.2%, 50%, 61.8%, and 100%.

To find a key Fibonacci ratio, you divide a number in the sequence by the following number and express it as a percentage. The Fibonacci sequence goes like this:

0,1,1,2,3,5,8,13,21,34...

Starting at the third number, we get 100% since we have 1/1. If you divide 21/34, you get 61.8%. Obviously, we are not using all of the ratios; there are certain ratios like 21/34 that are used by stock traders. Other ratios can be calculated by dividing a given number by a more distant, higher number in the sequence. For example, you can divide a number by one that is three places to the right. It is not understood how it works, but these numbers indicate price reversal points on stock charts.

The first step in learning how to use Fibonacci retracement is learning how to calculate the ratios. This is done in the following way. You take two extreme points on a stock chart in recent trading. In other words, you take a recent high price and a recent low price. Then, you calculate the vertical distance between the prices—in other words, just subtract the low price from the high price.

Once you have this distance, then you divide it by the key Fibonacci ratios.

Most computationally based stock charts actually allow you to put the key percentages on your stock charts as dashed horizontal lines. Thus, they will indicate the levels 0%, 23.6%, 38.2%, 50%, 61.8%, and 100% on your stock chart for you. Hence, you don't need to worry about doing any of the calculations—you can just eyeball the chart and then look for the stock price to hit one of these values. An example of this is shown below (from Wikipedia, using MetaTrader software):

The lines created by the Fibonacci ratios indicate possible levels of support and resistance. The percentage tells you how much the stock has moved as a price retracement. For example, in the graph above, we see a major drop in price all the way down to the 0% level, then there is a retracement of 38.2%. You will also notice that the 38.2%-line forms resistance in this case. However, it is considered that the stock or other financial asset is going to resume the prior trend once it hits a key Fibonacci ratio. In this case, there has been a major downtrend in the chart, and you can see on the far right of the chart, that it appears the downtrend is resuming.

The 50% level found by dividing 1/2 is used in the case of stocks because it is an important ratio for trend resumption. That is, if a stock does a 50% retracement, it is very likely to resume the previous trend.

It is important to take Fibonacci retracement with a grain of salt. Many analysists believe that any success found with Fibonacci retracement comes from a trader's own confirmation bias. However, more often than not (shall we say), the retracement levels found from the Fibonacci sequence do appear to work. This idea was popularized during the stock market boom in the movie "Pi," where a mathematical genius who studies the Fibonacci sequence supposedly discovers a secret formula that can generate huge returns on the stock market.

So while the Fibonacci sequence can indicate retracements and tell you when a trend is going to break or resume, you should definitely use this tool with care and avoid being seduced by it. It does not always give the right answers, and again, the way to use this tool with care is to use some of the other technical indicators that we have discussed in conjunction with it. The candlestick charts are considered to be one of the more reliable tools – so if you see a different signal with the candlestick patterns, the best way to proceed is to believe what the candlestick patterns are telling you rather than betting everything on the magic of the Fibonacci retracements.

Forex traders (currency exchange) tend to give Fibonacci retracements more weight than stock traders, although many stock traders do use this tool in their analysis.

Multiple Time Frames

A Fibonacci retracement is a tool that can be used on any time frame. Day traders sometimes use Fibonacci retracement, and in fact, Forex traders who are known as scalpers are known to use it. A scalper is a trader that actually trades on very short time frames, of minutes, in order to make very small profits. They hope to make it up by doing many trades throughout the day. Pennies add up to dollars as they say.

This technique is something that can definitely be used with swing trading. The phenomenon is going to be apparent no matter what time scale you are using. So you are going to see it on a daily time frame, a weekly time frame, and a monthly time frame.

This means that Fibonacci retracement is something that you can use no matter what trading style within Swing trading you adopt, and you can also use it when you are going to be doing outlying trades (that is you normally trade over 1-5 days, but find a 90-day trade to enter).

Takeaways

There are several key takeaways that we have when it comes to Fibonacci retracement. The first is that Fibonacci retracement levels can be used to identify likely pricing levels of support and resistance. This can be used to place your trades and identify points of exit.

While you can have your software simply draw the levels found by Fibonacci retracement on any stock market chart, you should have some basic understanding of where they come from. These levels have been identified as being relevant to the stock market through decades of experience of stock traders. The levels are found by dividing the distances in extreme stock prices on the chart. The levels are expressed as percentages found by dividing different numbers in the Fibonacci sequence. The percentages relevant to stock pricing appear to be 0%, 23.6%, 38.2%, 50%, 61.8%, and 100%. So 38.2% would indicate a 38.2% difference between a high and a low.

The Fibonacci retracement method may take on an air of infallibility because of its basis in high-level mathematics. However, you should not be taken in by this apparent magic. If you only rely on this method, you are likely to be misled into making bad trading decisions. You should use the Fibonacci retracement method in conjunction with other technical indicators and tools. This means having a solid familiarity with chart patterns, ABCD patterns, moving averages, candlestick charts, and other tools that you can use, such as the relative strength indicator.

And although this is not directly related, to avoid the unexpected, keep an eye on the financial news and the news generally at all times. Unexpected events can break all stock market patterns and suddenly send stock prices zooming high or crashing no matter what all the technical tools are telling you beforehand.

Chapter 9: A Brief Foray Into Fundamental Analysis

Fundamental analysis is a process of looking at a business at the most fundamental or basic level. Think about it this way. If your cousin came to you and said they had started a business and wanted you to invest, how would you make your investment decision? Character issues of your cousin aside, you'd want to know what products and services the company was offering, and then you'd want to dive into the company's financial data to see what it's revenue, growth, expenses, and debts are. You'd also evaluate the company for its future potential.

When it comes to companies on the stock market, this is all that fundamental analysis really is. You're going to be doing the same procedure on a large publicly traded company. This may even include personality evaluations. If your cousin is crazy, you might be tempted by the business idea, but hold off on investing because you feel that your cousin would not be a good business manager. With publicly traded companies, investors might do the same if they don't like the board or management team, or just the CEO.

One of the debates among swing traders is whether or not they should use fundamental analysis or not. The truth is, that depends on the time horizons that you use in your trading. Since there are many different trading styles in swing trading, not all swing traders are going to be using fundamental analysis. However, fundamental analysis can be used by swing traders. If you are going to be holding your positions for weeks or months at a time, then doing a bit of fundamental analysis is going to be helpful in producing winning trades.

Even short-term traders should be doing some fundamental analysis. Do you have to dig into it to the degree that a Warren Buffet would? Of course not – however, knowing what the company is up to and its financial health can help you choose better trades.

Swing trading generally doesn't require in-depth fundamental analysis. Unlike a long-term investor, you are not tying yourself to the company. However, you may want to do fundamental analysis in order to get a solid handle on the company's fortunes, especially on a quarter-to-quarter basis. Remember that a company that is solid when it comes to fundamental analysis is going to be attracting a lot of investment, including big investment houses. As a swing trader, you can take advantage of this as well, because that can push up stock prices.

One way that you can use fundamental analysis is to find companies that are going to be undergoing a long trend. If a company is posting solid numbers, it might have an ongoing uptrend in share price that can last weeks, a quarter, or even up to a year or more. Using the trade with the trend philosophy, these kinds of steadily rising stocks can provide profit opportunities for swing traders that are patient enough to wait out longer trades.

Earnings calls are generally to be avoided, in my opinion, but some do find opportunity there. These often result in major price swings. The problem with them is that before the fact, people are speculating without any real data to back up their beliefs. That makes getting in on a trade before an earning call a difficult proposition. One way to get around it is to hedge your bet. Hence, if the speculation is that a company is going to be reporting a good earnings call that is going to result in a large increase in share price, you can buy a lot of shares—but hedge your bet by also shorting the stock with a smaller bet so that you can cap your losses if there is a downturn instead.

There is the option of waiting until after the earnings call to make a move on the stock. This can work, but you need to be aware that there are many difficulties. The first is that you are going to have a very hard time getting in on a trade at the opening bell under these circumstances. The price of a stock can be rising or falling very fast if expectations are "exceeded," so fast that it might be hard for individual traders to execute a trade. You might have to place a limit order offering a higher price than you would really like to pay for the stock.

A second problem that sometimes arises in these situations is that in many cases, the rise or fall that is going to happen with a stock happens extremely quickly, and then after that, there is a long consolidation period. So you might miss the boat entirely, and sometimes the boat leaves the harbor in after-hours trading.

Since this is a book about swing trading, we are not going to cover fundamental analysis in detail, but we will give readers an overview of how they can use some level of fundamental analysis in their evaluations of companies that are good to trade.

Earnings And Cash Flow

The first thing you are going to want to look at for a company is the state of its cash flow. You are not going to be looking into investing in companies for the long-term as a swing trader, so you are not interested in the long-term financial health of the company, per se. But remember that many other investors are interested in such things. So a company with good cash flow, in particular, good net income that is increasing YOY, is going to be a company that is attracting a lot of investors. That, in turn, means that the company is going to be one that sees the stock prices pushed up.

Earnings are the most important factor with any company, but you need to look at some specific measures. One of these is earnings per share. This gives you the amount of profit the company is making per share, and this is something that can be compared from stock to stock. Keep in mind that you will want to compare apples to apples, so if you are looking at EPS, be sure to make comparisons between companies that are in similar sectors.

The price to earnings ratio is another important measure. This will help you determine if a stock is over or underpriced, given the fundamentals of the company. A company with a certain level of profitability that has a low P/E ratio is a stock that can be expected to rise at some point. These are the kinds of companies that a Warren Buffet may target, but you can target them also. Again, compare P/E ratios in a given sector. A technology company, for example, can be expected to have a high P/E ratio.

PEG or projected earnings growth is an estimate of the future growth rate of the stock. If this is a good number, this can indicate that this could be a stock you can profit from using a 90- to 180-day swing trade.

Price to book ratio helps you gauge the real value of the company. "Book value" is the value of the company on the books. You don't have to be an accountant to use it, most stock market sites publish the calculated values, and you can compare to like companies. If it is low, this could be a company that may enter an uptrend.

Other Factors

You will also want to take a look at the company's balance sheets and income statements. In particular, you want to see two things, in my opinion. The first is how much debt the company is taking on. Take a look at this, especially if the company pays dividends. If a company is taking on a large amount of debt, it is going to have less ability to pay dividends in the coming months. Dividends are a factor in attracting many investors, and if a company that pays dividends goes into a lot of debt, investors may end up dumping the stock. Just something to be aware of.

One situation to key in on is a company that had good revenue but a bad earnings report because of rising expenses. This often happens because the company has made investments that are going to improve its performance in the future. Thus, the one-time investments may reduce profits in the current quarter, but over the coming 90 to 180 days, the company is going to see improved profitability—and hence much higher stock prices—due to the fact that they won't have to make the investments again (at least, not in the short term) and that actual profits will grow. Thus, keep your eye on companies that are known to be profitable that might have a disappointing earnings report. Do the research to find out why, and if a company had bad earnings because it is devoting funds to investments for the future, it could be a good trade.

Conclusion

Thank you for making it through to the end of **Swing Trading Secrets**! Let's hope it was informative and able to provide you with all of the tools you need to achieve your goals.

Swing trading offers you an opportunity to start a stock trading business and earn real profits. Unlike day trading, you can get started with swing trading by working on it part-time and with a small amount of capital. You can grow your business over time and move slowly up to bigger trades as you earn more profits.

Swing trading takes advantage of the natural ups and downs (or price swings) that always occur in the market. Every single trading day, there are opportunities to earn profits by trading the price swings. You have learned everything you need to get started with swing trading:

- Time frames or time intervals for various trading styles

- Different candlestick charts that swing traders use

- ABCD charts and Gartley patterns, as well as patterns that indicate trend reversals

- Stop-loss and take-profit levels

- Technical indicators, including moving averages and the Relative Strength Indicator (RSI)

- And much more!

The time is now to start your swing trading business and begin earning profits. If you don't have a brokerage account, get going and open one. You can start swing trading doing small trades to get started. Thousands of dollars are not required. In the beginning, keep reinvesting your profits until you get to the point where you can begin taking out an income while maintaining enough funds to continue trading.

Thank you again for purchasing this book!

Reviews are crucial if a book can thrive Amazon or simply dies out. Hence our success as authors and publishers heavily depends on them. So if you found this book useful in any way, I would be delighted to see a review from you with your feedback on what you liked and what can be improved.

Thank you so much!

Printed in the USA
CPSIA information can be obtained
at www.ICGtesting.com
LVHW010234110324
774109LV00010B/743